Source of Inspiration Vol. 10

Inspirational Poems
From: *Source of Inspiration*

Website: **www.patcegan.wordpress.com**

Copyright © 2017 Patricia E. Cegan

All rights reserved. No part of this publication may be used for commercial gain. However, readers may reproduce and distribute for the sole purpose of sharing the inspiration of these Source poems. Should you wish to use this series of inspirational poetry for fund raising purposes for charitable causes, please contact Ms. Cegan at the email address below:

E-mail: patcegan@hotmail.com

ISBN 10:   9781077980228

TABLE OF CONTENTS

- TRAITS OF BEAUTY 1
- THOSE IN NEED 1
- BEAUTIFUL? 1
- MY FIRE 2
- YOURS 2
- NEVER JUST ONE 3
- COMIC BOOK LIVING 3
- JUST RIGHT 4
- BUBBLE GUM BUBBLES 5
- NO! 5
- IF ONLY 6
- OTHER SIDE OF THE STREET 7
- THE PERFECT PEARL 8
- BINGO 8
- PERHAPS 9
- THE PERFUME OF YOUR NEARNESS 9
- USED TO BE FREE 10
- LOST PRECIOUS CHANCES 10
- HALLOWEEN EVERY DAY 11
- UNCONQUERABLE 11
- OPEN DOORS 12
- OUR BIRTHRIGHT 13
- BLINK 13
- ANOTHER WORLD 14
- THE GIFT OF NEED 14
- UNDESERVED BLESSINGS 15

HOLY	16
READY FOR WISDOM	16
GOD'S BLESSING	16
MOLDED BY OUR CREATOR	16
GIFT OF GOD	17
GIFTS FOUND IN OPPOSITES	17
ONLY	18
FOCUS ON THE LORD	18
RIVERS OF SORROW	19
WHY PRAISE GOD?	20
GRACIOUS RECEIVER	21
INDEPENDENT	22
LANGUAGE OF LOVE	23
THROW-AWAY WORLD	23
LITTLE COG TRAIN	24
DIVIDE	24
LIFE'S SECRET	25
TIME'S ILLUSION	26
UNITED IN PRAYER	26
GOD OF MERCY	27
TWO BY TWO	28
ON MY WAY	29
WHERE AM I?	30
IDLE CHATTER	30
I AM FREE	31
NO QUESTIONS	32
WHAT COST?	32

MAGIC OR MIRACLES	33
MAKE DO	34
FRAGILE FRIENDS	34
CLARITY	35
CHANGING ROLES	35
WHERE'S HOME?	35
DO I BELIEVE?	36
MIRACLES	37
BREAKING CHAINS	37
SILENT CONVERSATIONS	38
A RUSHING WIND	40
STEPPING OUT OF LIFE	40
PARTY-LINE TELEPHONES	41
ALONG THE WAY	42
BEGINS WITH ME	42
RUBE'S CUBE	43
POLISHED TO PERFECTION	43
FIND YOUR JOY	44
NOT A VICTIM	45
LITTLE OR A LOT	46
GOD GAVE ME LIFE	46
FREE IN A PRISON	47
EXPLOSIONS	47
APOLOGIES	48
TAKE ME	49
SWEET MYSTERY	49
KEEPING FOCUSED	50

ECHOES	50
BEGIN	51
CLIMBING	51
KEEP FOCUSED	52
FRUIT	52
FALL	53
YOUR INNER BEING	53
MORE THAN A RESERVOIR	54
UNCHANGING HEART OF LOVE	54
THE DREAMER	55
HOW MANY TRUTHS?	56
GIVE AND TAKE	56
SOUND THE HORN	57
ICE CREAM	58
MY GOD OF LOVE	58
SACRED CHILDHOOD	59
THE UGLINESS OF HYPOCRISY	60
WAS I KIND TODAY?	60
SERVICE	61
BE OF GOOD CHEER	61
ON FIRE	62
FORGOTTEN PROMISE	62
SPECIAL MOMENTS	63
FAIRY TALES	64
MORE THAN ONE	64
THE ART OF LIVING WELL	64
AGAIN	66

MY BODY	67
PRIORITIES	67
DARKNESS TO LIGHT	68
READY?	69
SERENITY	70
SEE-SAW	71
MISTAKES	71
COMES AND GOES	71
TIMES OF CRISIS	72
WHO AM I?	72
MAN OF GREATNESS	73
PLANTING DREAMS	73
THE TAP ROOT	74
OUR WISDOM	75
NOTHING'S IMPOSSIBLE	75
PIONEER OF FAITH	76
GOD'S PLAN	76
FAITH GROWS	78
NO NEED TO SHOUT	78
WAIT	79
I BELIEVE	79
THE MARK	80
VALUE OF PRAYER	81
WHO IS MY JUDGE?	82
STORMS OF ANGER	83
HE IS HAPPY	83
WITHIN INFINITY	84

HIGHER AND HIGHER	85
ANGELS SING	85
PETER PAN PUPPY	86
HOUR BEFORE DAWN	86
MY DUTY?	87
NOT THE WISEST	88
ONLY ME	89
OLD	90
FREE?	90
BITTER ON THE TONGUE	91
OLD-FASHIONED VIRTUES	91
WHITE LIES	91
PRETTY POEMS	91
ARE YOU KIND?	92
WHO STARTED IT?	92
SIMPLY SIMPLE	93
SO BUSY	93
GOODBYE TO GLOOM	94
WOVEN IN WOE	94
WHEN?	95
BUBBLE DREAMS	95
NEXT MORNING REGRETS	95
THINKING	96
MY ANCHOR	96
SEA BREEZES	97
SO RARE	97
WALKING TO NOWHERE	97

DOING GOD'S WILL	98
ELASTIC DREAMS	98
LOVELINESS OF FAITH	99
OPINIONS!	99
JUST LAUGH	100
GREAT	100
DANCE OF RIBBONS	101
TODAY'S LAUGH	101
BODY DRUMMING	101
CAR GAMES	102
MORNING MANTRAS	102
SNEAKY CAT	103
NO EASY WAY	103
MISTLETOE KISS	104
LEAN ON ME	104
IN THE SILENCE OF PRAYER	105
HIDDEN FIRE	105
REVERENCE	106
TAKING	106
MORE	107
PRETTY POEMS	107
WALKING IN FAITH	107
THE PERFECT LIFE	108
SUMMER FUN	108
MIRROR'S TRUTH	108
LEAVE ROOM FOR FAITH	109
WHEN I WANT TO QUIT	109

BACKSLIDER	110
CALL IN THE CLOWNS	111
A ROSE	111
COURTESY	112
PEARLS OF GRACE	112
CALL IN THE CLOWNS	113
LOVE IS A VERB	113
MEEK AND HUMBLE	114
GUILTY I AM	115
TIME TO STOP	115
GETTING STRONGER	116
A THING OF BEAUTY	117
A PASSING GLANCE	118
HALF-A-HEALTH NUT	118
AT LEAST I TRY	119
WEARY AM I	119
REFLECTIONS	120
WONDER	121
SUNSET REFLECTIONS	121
WORRY FREE	121
MYSTERY	122
THUS DIVINE	123
EXPECTATION	123
FORGOTTEN SHOE	124
ALLOWING LIFE'S MYSTERIES	125
THE VOID	125
THE IMMENSITY OF GOD	126

THE FLOWER	126
ALL TO COME	126
LOST GOD	127
AT LAST AT PEACE	128
WORRY FREE	129
PIANO	129
LAST CHANCE	130
SPRIGS OF JOY	130
TONGUELESS SILENCE	131
THE RACE IS ON	132
A TINY HAND	133
ANGEL OF PRAYER	133
WHAT MONEY CAN'T BUY	134
LIFE'S SWEETNESS	134
LAST LEAF	135
LIPS	135
HOW TO BE	135
BATTLE OF THE BULGE	136
TOO OLD TO LEARN	137
RUNNING IN CIRCLES	138
NO FRIEND	138
TAKE A BOW	139
MAKING A LIST	139
SKIPPING STILL	139
NO MORE GOSSIP	140
NOT GOING TO HELL	140
SEA HORSE MAGIC	140

SUNRISE MIRACLE	141
TRUTH-TELLING	141
KNIGHT OF GOOD DEEDS	142
REMEMBERING GOD	143
DESPAIR	143
PUNISH?	144
COUNTRY FAIR	144
MAKING A HOUSE A HOME	144
CANDLES IN THE WINDOWS	145
ALCHEMY OF ERROR	145
TOO NEAT	146
SHOWER SONGS	146
DIET, RULE #1	146
WORKING HARD	146
NO BAD NEWS	147
TAKE CONTROL OF YOUR LIFE	148
DON'T HELP A FOOL	148
DON'T HOLD ON TO ENVY	148
THE INCONVENIENCE OF POVERTY	149
SELF-LOVE	149
STEADFASTNESS OF THE LORD	150
WEED TO FLOWER	150
MY WEALTH	151
PLEASING PEOPLE	151
THE HOLINESS OF PRAYER	151
PLANTING A SEED	152
GRANDMOTHER'S TABLE	153

SUMMER TREAT	153
WAIT TO MARRY	153
OLD AGE	153
CREAKY YOGA	154
BATHROOM LIBRARY	154
MORNING LAUGH	154
NEVER LATE	154
THY WILL	155
SOUR PUSS	156
DREAMS OF MY HEART	156
YOUR PRESENCE	156
WON'T TRY	157
SURROUND AND WITHIN	157
BECOMING YOU	157
PARADE	158
NOT THE SAME	158
KIND FLOWERS	159
UNMEASURABLE	159
LIFE'S RUT	159
TEENAGE LAMENT	160
WATCH YOUR LANGUAGE	161
WORDS OF TRUTH	161
A HEALTHY TONGUE	161
ROLLER COASTER RIDE	162
LIVE	162
WHAT MIGHT HAVE BEEN	163
A LOVING HEART	163

THE GAME	164
POWER OF LOVE	164
HOLIDAYS	165
POWER OF SILENT PRAYER	165
EMPTY PRAYERS	166
ALL HOURS	166
YOUR SILENT HEART	167
HEAVENLY FRAGRANCE	167
CHOOSE WELL	168
MOUSE IN THE HOUSE	169
STARS OF GOOD DEEDS	169
BROKEN PROMISES	170
DON'T SETTLE FOR LESS	170
GOLDEN IDOLS	171
LIVING WATERS	172
NO DARKNESS IN THE LIGHT	172
LORD'S DAY	173
ENDLESS CHATTER	174
THINGS I CAN'T STAND	175
IMPOSSIBLE	175
NO TIME	176
A DOT	176
SILENT DESPERATION	177
LONELY IN CROWDS	177
WHERE I GO	178
STOP DOING IT	179
GOD SPEAKS TO US	180

WORLD OF MUSIC	181
GONE ASTRAY	182
FADE AWAY	183
NOT MY JOB	183
BEWARE OF THE TRICKSTER	184
LONGING FOR PEACE	185
LEARNING TO LOVE	185
NICE	186
RAINBOWS	187
TRAPPED?	187
INTERNAL DIALOGUE	188
IT'S YOUR FAULT	189
GOD AT PLAY	189
GOD KNOWS	190
EMBROIDERY LESSON	190
HOUSEWORK THERAPY	190
MAMA'S ANSWER	190
AUTUMN	191
LOVE VERSUS JUDGEMENT	191
CLAIMING OUR IDOLS	192
ENVY TO INSPIRATION	192
HOW WE PERCEIVE	193
FEAR AND DOUBT	193
BOYS VERSUS GIRLS	194
LOVE ME AS I AM	194
TOMATOES	194
CANDLES	195

MORE STUFF?	195
CAN'T SEE HIM	196
SENDING OUT	196
TODAY	197
HALLOWEEN	197
SYMBOLS	197
DON'T KNOW	198
CAN'T SLEEP	199
WHAT IS PRAISE?	199
DOING THE BEST I CAN	200
DO DREAMS COME TRUE?	201
MY GOD IS LOVE	202
LITTLE LESSONS	203
SOUP	203
PICKLES	203
PLAYFUL MELODIES	204
WHO IS RIGHT?	204
HAPPY OR SAD	205
NOTHING IS MINE	206
ON TIP TOES	206
WINDING DOWN	207
ONE WORD POEM	208
PLAY	208
THROUGH THE VALLEY OF DEATH	208
SLEEP	209
AGAIN	210
EXCEPT WHEN I DON'T	210

HOPE OR FAITH	212
WHY I FORGIVE	213
LOST TEARS	213
LOVE ME?	213
LOVE ON A STICK	215
OPEN THE WINDOW	215
WHO YOU ARE	216
INTEGRITY?	217
LOVE SIGNALS	217
BROKEN PROMISES	217
TRUE FAILURE	217
MAYBE—THE LIE	218
WHICH ONE?	218
PEOPLE PLEASING	218
LOWER YOUR EYES	218
WHAT'S THE DIFFERENCE?	219
STUBBORN	220
IMPOSSIBLE	220
HARDEN HEART	221
WHAT'S THE DIFFERENCE?	222
ONE MORE	222
HOW GOSSIP STARTS	223
JUSTICE	223
THE PENALTY	223
WHO ME?	223
WHEN DO WE FINISH?	224
EXACTLY	225

BUY MORE	225
TAPPING	225
EVIL—PART OF THE PLAN?	226
FORGET IT	227
NEVER SAY NEVER	227
SMILING FACES	228
EMPATHY	228
COMMUNICATING WITH THE SOUL	228
A MOMENT IN TIME	229
YOUR FULL ATTENTION	229
BEHIND THE WALL	230
WHAT'S COMING?	231
CHAINS OF FEAR	231
I AM LIGHT	232
INDISCRIMINATE LOVE?	233
WHAT STEALS YOUR JOY?	234
MOST FRAGILE TIMES	235
HOW BIG	236
THE CACTUS	236
WHO I REALLY AM	236
BEYOND THE VEIL	237
BECOMING MY DOG	237
NOISE	238
FROM THE LORD	238
IN AND OUT	239
YOU POKED MY HEART	240
FROM THE LORD	241

NOT READY	241
LORD, CLOSE MY MOUTH	242
GOING, GOING, GONE	242
ONE AT A TIME	243
MY SHOES	244
BLUE	244
DOGGIE BAG	245
NO PEACE ON EARTH	245
PAINT A PICTURE	245
HE IS LIGHT	246
I—THE ENEMY	246
THE PRISONER	247
THE BUBBLE	247
SAD POEM	248
OUR MEMORIAL	248
A LITTLE HONEST	249
WINTER'S GIFT	250
HOLOGRAMS OF GOD	250
SLEEPING DOGS	250
ANOTHER TIME	251
COLD FEET	251
KNOWLEDGE WITHOUT GOD	251
ONE LITTLE CANDLE	252
SIMPLE MATH	253
SOURCE OF LIGHT	253
NO EXPLANATION NEEDED	254
GOING TO MARKET	255

FINALLY	255
WALKING THAT LINE	256
BLEEDING	256
PUSH AND PULL	257
GOING HOME	257
SOON	258
I PROMISE	258
CHATTERBOX HEAD	259
RELIGION FOR SALE	259
BABIES AND DOGS	260
OUR INTEGRITY	261
CAT-IN-THE-LAP	262
VIOLENT GAMES	262
WITCHES RIDING	262
PRETENDING	262
LABELS	263
NO EXPLANATION NEEDED	263
RESPECT ALL	263
WHY DO GOOD	263
DO YOU CARE?	264
NO HOME	265
NEW BEGINNINGS	266
DANCING IN THE MOONLIGHT	266
THINGS I KNOW	267
TIME TO GO	267
NO NAME	268
TOO MANY BOOKS	269

WHAT I AM AND AM NOT	269
LESS AND LESS	270
REAFFIRM OUR GOODNESS	271
NO DEFINITION	272
JUST ONE LITTLE CANDLE	273
SINS OF OLD	274
PICKLE POEM	274
GARDEN OF SORROW	275
NEVER FORGIVE	275
DISRESPECT	276
FINALLY FREE	276
THE HAT	276
WHO CAN I TRUST?	277
DAY OF REST	277
STONED	277
1000 CUTS	278
P-NUT BUTTER	278
TWIST OF FATE	278
LORD, GIVE ME A HAND	279
HUMBLE HEART	280
FOLLOW THE CROWD	280
TO MOTHERHOOD	281
RESPECT	282
THOSE IN NEED	282
A MOMENT IN TIME	283
LIFE'S GIFTS	283
YOUR GRACE, YOUR MIRACLE	284

JUST TRY	285
NO SAINT NOR SAGE	285
IN MUSIC	286
SEEK TO GROW	287
GIFT OF SCENT	288
PEOPLE	288
MAGIC CARPET	289
HOW LONG DOES IT TAKE?	289
NOT YOU, NOT ME	290
HOW WE "SHOULD" FEEL	290
I'M AFRAID	291
EXACTLY WHO YOU ARE	291
NEW COMMITMENTS	291
UNCHANGING TRUTH	292
NO HATE	293
CHOCOLATE KISSES	294
A HAVEN	294
HALO OF GOLD	294
FOREVER FREE	295
GOD'S MERCY	295
HEAD NOISE	296
CREATOR OF ALL	297
DROP OF WATER	297
GOD IS	298
PREPARING FOR WAR	298
POINT OF VIEW	299
JUST AS IT IS	299

HOLY MOMENTS	300
LEAVE THE REST TO GOD	300
TIME OF BEFORE	301
DRAGONFLY RIDE	301
MAGIC AND DREAMS	302
LIVING MY LIFE AGAIN	303
MY JOB, MY WORK	304
THE GYPSY GIRL	305
GREEN	306
DON'T SAY "I LOVE YOU"	306
FREE WILL?	307
NO SEE, NO HEAR	307
WOLF IN DISGUISE	308
TORMENTOR OR TEACHER?	309
MORE THAN EMPTY WORDS	309

Traits of Beauty

The traits of true beauty
can be described
by the qualities
of virtue, for who
can be beautiful
without being
generous, kind, compassionate
modest, innocent, honest?

Beauty is found
not in Photo Shop design
but rather coming from
a heart overflowing
with love.

Those in Need

Helping those in need
Helps us learn compassion
Gives us gratitude

Beautiful?

I see you as beautiful
are you really
or do I see only
what my heart shows me?

My Fire

You are my fire
my one desire
my heart is Yours
forever more.

Oh, the sweet passion
of youth which
evolves into
the sublime with time
expanding my ability
to love the One
who remains my fire.

Yours

I am Yours
Your willing servant
humbled by Your love
awed by Your glory.

Shooting stars above
fireflies below
twinkles of light
on dew-kissed morning webs.

Light reins supreme
darkness fades away

bathe me in Your light
that I may become
a beacon of Your love.

Never Just One

Candy kisses
sweet, melting, delicious
eating one that tastes like "more."
The secret of restraint
is to never have the first
somehow, I never remember.

Comic Book Living

Pow, wow, comic book action
cartoon life
Charlie Brown, Pig Pen
make-believe stories

Books filed high
fairies fill the sky
Is life real
or stories told
again and again
humanity spiraling
toward its
own destruction?

Tattoos, body piercing

hey, somebody
notice me
care if I'm alive
never knowing
the soul inside
too busy looking
for what we already have
a connection with the Divine
that lifts us out of the illusion
into the Great Beyond.

Just Right

Too much, too little
Goldilocks looking
for what's just right
never satisfied
too hot, too cold
too hard, too soft
she wanders
never satisfied
never knowing
a happy end
passing by it
again and again.

What is this longing
of the soul
that keeps us searching
for what's
"just right?"

Bubble Gum Bubbles

Bubble gum bubbles
Bigger and bigger they grow
The game ends with "pop!"

No!

No
seems like a simple word
when it's actually a time-bomb
of "what ifs"…
they get mad
don't love me anymore
leave me all alone
afraid, undefended
hugless

Hell, is there
anybody out there?
All I said was
one tiny "no."

If Only

If my belly was flat
everyone would love me

if only my thighs were firm
hair was curly
teeth straight
somebody would be
my friend.

If I could sing
stood up taller
had brown eyes not green
tell me, God
why did you make
me so inferior
when I could have been
richer, more beautiful
smarter, happier?

Why all the imperfections
hard life, then I die?
Such a tragedy
oh, poor me!

Other Side of the Street

I woke up
that's a good beginning
some day I won't
I'm grateful for a cozy bed
birds singing outside
my window
my dog snuggling
next to me
giving little wet kisses

If my day starts so sweetly
imagine how wonderful
the rest will be.

Two sides of the street
one filled with serenity
one with chaos.
The houses on both sides
look the same
but what goes on
within are worlds apart.

I used to live on the other side
complaining all the time
but I moved across the street
where life is filled with
gratitude and serenity.
Won't you come
live with me?

The Perfect Pearl

A gain of sand
inside a shell
irritates until
the oyster begins
to cover the sand
with luminescent colors
forming a perfect pearl.

How I wish I could do that

    transform each irritant
    into a beautiful
    pearl of wisdom.

    Oh, but you can, my child
    Just layer it with love
    and soon you will have
    another perfect pearl.

Bingo

B egin each day with prayer
I nvite God into your heart
N ever lose an opportunity to be kind
G o the second mile
O perate with love at all times.

Perhaps

P eople afraid to make a decision
E ach time one could fail
R egret for past mistakes is strong
H ow can I be sure the decision is "right"
A lways things could go wrong
P erhaps tomorrow I'll decide
S afe is he who procrastinates

    or so he thinks!

The Perfume of Your Nearness

I awake to the perfume
of Your nearness
go to sleep wrapped in
Your love.

There is never a time
when You are not with me
only times when I carelessly
forget the nearness
of Your heart
until You once again
whisper
I am here
now and forever more.

Used to be Free

Will we soon have to buy
sunshine in a plastic bottle
all natural, no smog?
Seems to me
we shouldn't have to
pay to pee
or for a glass of water
somethings should
always be free.

Lost Precious Chances

How many precious chances
have passed away
days spent in gloom
sad hearts filled with woe
laughter long forgotten?

Even one is too many
for each night we are
renewed in slumber
at sunrise our souls
awaken to a new day.

Rejoice for our many blessings
count them one-by-one
let even sorrow become
a blessing
spread joy where're you go.

Happiness is a choice.

Halloween Every Day

Fortitude, perseverance, courage
old-fashioned virtues some say
modesty, purity, honesty
thrown away with corsets
replaced by tattoos, body piercing
strobe lights, blue hair

It's Halloween every day now

Devils everywhere
I can't make this leap
so remain
an old fashioned girl.

Unconquerable

Complaints are thick
as blackberries
self-pity is found
everywhere
courage as rare
as truth

Yet, in the center
of creation
one finds our Lord
telling us
we are unconquerable
with Him by our side.
We shall arrive
in His good time
changing failure
to lessons learned
and fear to faith.

Open Doors

Open all your windows and doors
let everything pass in and

out freely, even evil.

Do not be afraid of truth
let it come easier
than a lie
welcome truth
for with it comes
the light of love
in which no darkness
can remain.

Our Birthright

The Divine within
is available to all
yet not all
open their hearts
to this gift.

Fear, suspicion, indifference
willfulness, disbelief
keep us from receiving
this joyous presence
with patiently waits
until we are ready
to accept this birthright
of love from
the Creator of all
that is pure and good.

Blink

Blink, a life-time gone
Waste not one precious moment
Grateful for it all

Another World

I live in another world
separate from where
my body roams
I seek nothing from this world
not recognition, wealth
or admiration.

I am not a saint
though I am sacred
for I hold the
remembrance of God
at all times
for He is in me
and I am part of Him.

The Gift of Need

What a gift of need
which, having exhausted
my options, I finally
am forced to turn
to God.

Tears of yearning
flood my eyes
I am filled
with helplessness
I stretch my hands
up in supplication.

Immediately is my soul
flooded with the deep
sea of light and love.
"I am here, my child
ever at your side.
You need only to desire
My presence for it
to be revealed to you."

I weep in gratitude
for the need that
forces me out of my
complacency
into the arms
of our loving God.

Undeserved Blessings

Blessing
often in disguise
ignored, undeserved
yet given freely
by He who is
our God of love.

Holy

H e who walks in the light
O ne with the Lord
L ove lights his path
Y ou can be holy, too

Ready for Wisdom

Wisdom
comes from grace
a blessing to be shared
for those ready to receive

God's Blessing

Paint the skies with joy
Spread to all who are in need
Joy is God's blessing

Molded by Our Creator

I am who I am
I need be no other
Molded by our loving Creator

I am who I'm supposed to be

Gift of God

Give me the gift of silence
in which I may hear
the songs of angels
who guide me
silence
contains opportunity
to hear the voice
of God

Gifts Found in Opposites

Look to the opposite
for the gifts are
often found there
gain from loss
wealth in poverty
strength in weakness
for only is the pinnacle
reached when starting
from the lowest point.

In my powerlessness
do I finally reach out
for the Lord for His
mercy is everlasting
to he who calls His name.

Only

> Only in deprivation
> did I learn to give
> only I sorrow
> did my heart fill
> with compassion
>
> Great is my God
> who gives me strength
> His mercy fills
> my soul with
> the Light of His Love.

Focus on the Lord

> Keep you focus
> on our Creator
> allowing all else
> to fade away
>
> Walk in silent prayer
> open to receive
> what the Lord
> deems to give
>
> Be at peace
> for only in serenity
> do you find

the power of the Lord

Rivers of Sorrow

How does one stop
rivers of resentment
tides of judgment
oceans of regret?

Alone, one is trapped
in frail thoughts
sighs, tears of woe.
But he who calls
in supplication
to be released
by God's mercy
moves into the realm
of Divine inspiration
leaving behind
transgressions
and sorrow.

Blessed is He
who lifts us up
into the lap of love
His mercy is
everlasting.

Why Praise God?

Praise God
but why?
Certainly not for Him
rather to remind us
of His mercy, generosity
His all-encompassing love
for us, His creation.

Love God
but how?
How do we love
that which we
cannot see?
Faith comes from
His grace which
He generously bestows.

Fear God
but why would we
need to fear
a God of pure love?

For me, fear
changes to awe
at the grandeur
of God
the sheer enormity
of His creation
the precision
beauty of this world.

Awe, I stand in awe

of my Creator
who is within
my soul
guiding me
loving me
for now and ever more.

Gracious Receiver

Magic words
when spoken in truth
yet how often our pride
binds our tongue

"I'm sorry"
spoken with intent
to not repent the error
heals both he who says
these magic words
and he who is
a gracious receiver.

Independent

I always took pride
in being independent
don't need anyone
do it myself

The years are teaching me
that at times, I do
need others
and I need
to be generous enough
to accept help
from others
so they can receive
the gifts of compassion
generosity
patience
that helping others
provides.

O, Lord, help me
put away pride
selfishness
teach me
how to love someone
who is being blessed
by helping me.

Help me to be
a gracious receiver.

Language of Love

Purse
holder of coins and small trinkets
purse

my lips to whistle and blow coffee
language is so ambiguous
no wonder we have trouble
communication at times

Yet the language of pure love
is universal
connecting us all
God has created
for in the end
there is only love

Throw-away World

Don't fix
throw away
make to break
so we have to buy more

Mountains of cast-offs
resources depleted
all is polluted
earth, water, sky
stop this insanity
before we all die

Little Cog Train

Chug-chug-chug
little train going uphill

cog wheels keep
the train on track
one cog at a time

One step at a time
secured by the cog
of God's love
we make our way
through life
we need not worry
about tomorrow
keep our focus
on now
for God is ever with us
one cog at a time

Divide

Divide
multiply, share
become many who
return to One
wiser, kinder
for learning to share
a step toward love

Life's Secret

Proclaim
shout it from the house tops

let it be known
so simple is the message
that no one pays attention
until they hear its whisper
deep within their hearts.

Let all you do
say
think
be based
on love.

So simple
we can't believe it.
Life is about
learning to love.

Time's Illusion

T icking away our lives
I maging its unlimited
M eandering with no purpose
E nding with regrets

T hankful for each moment
I nvesting our time wisely
M aking our lives full of loving purpose
E ach day an opportunity to serve the Lord

Time, life's illusion
speed it up, slow it down
but it never stands still

yet, at times, it seems to disappear
as I move into another reality

Time, neither friend nor foe
for it's only a false concept
for all exists throughout eternity
with momentary flickers
of attention
which soon are gone

United in Prayer

Sound the horn
call to prayer
join millions
across the globe
who stop their busy lives
to give thanks
connect to the Divine
and to each other.

What if this beautiful custom
was practiced each day
regardless of beliefs
how powerful is the loving voice
of seven million people
united in prayer
throughout the day?

Mountains would move
peace would reign
we would finally understand

we are all one.

God of Mercy

O God of mercy
the sweet divine
others paint You
as vengeful
a god who has favorites
but I know You
only as love
compassion, patience

There is none but He
and He is Love.

Two by Two

Two by two
into the ark
very few know
how to be alone
yet it is in these
moments of solitude
when finally we grow quiet
that we can best hear
that voice within
guiding us
teaching us
showing us how to live

a meaning full life.

I take time to be alone
quiet, ready to receive
open in sweet surrender
it always comes
the loving presence
of He who speaks to us
in the depths of our hearts

My eyes fill with tears
of gratitude
my heart beats a steady
pulse of love.
I am with my lord
who fills me
with serenity
for now and ever more.

On My Way

I'm on my way
but where am I going?
Am I sure I want
to be there when I arrive
for surely if I keep going
where I'm going
I will arrive there someday.*

Do we really consider where
our actions will lead

or are we just blundering
through life in pin-ball fashion?

What do you need to do
to feel you have had the life
you wanted when you
reach the end?

A question worth asking.

*Adapted from a Navajo sage's advice

Where Am I?

Where am I
here, there, anywhere?
Are there any absolutes
realities, truths?
I live in
an Alice in Wonderland World
ups are downs, downs are up
the Emperor has no clothes
but everyone says he does.
Is there anyone out there?
I find this world
more than a little crazy.
Am I the only one who does?

Idle Chatter

Idle chatter
empty words that never cease
what if we could only speak
to encourage or teach
something a person
could not learn on their own?
How quiet the world would be.
What if only words
spoken were from a loving heart?
Would there be any sounds heard?

I Am Free

I am free
from my past
no resentment, shame or regret
what will I think about all day?

I am free
of my worry about the future
no "what-ifs" any more
What will I think about
all day?

So many hours
filled with yesterdays
and fearful tomorrows
that I seldom pay
close attention
to what's happening

right now.

Yet, now is all
there is
but really
what is now?

No Questions

Can one write poetry
or live life without
asking questions?
Can we just accept
what is happening
right now without
why, who, what or when?

Whatever is occurring
will reveal itself
and if not
it is not the time
to know.

Difficult idea
for me who is
always so full of questions.

What Cost?

What is the cost
what will we pay?
We can do whatever we want
but it's never free
not even for a day.

Magic or Miracles

Magic or miracles
illusion or real
but now even
reality shifts
or perhaps
it always did.

Memories alter
over time or
simply fade away

The body slowing down
the mind slipping stiches
we unravel until
only a thread remains
until finally it disengages, too.

But the soul, if such
a thing exists
where is it in this decline
off to glory
into hell
or does it simply
cease to be?

Make Do

Recycle, reuse, make do
don't replace, renew.
If we don't stop wasting
soon there will be
no me or you!

Fragile Friends

Here I am
now I am not
I may not pass
this way again
just an annoying fly
that used to be
your friend.

You've pulled away
I know not why
as I watch
our friendship die
perhaps somewhere
Sometime we'll meet again
and you will be my friend.

Clarity

Believe
but if you don't
ask for clarity
faith with good intent
if still you don't
believe it's okay
it may not be
a truth for you
yours will come some day

Changing Roles

People, animals
where do we draw the line
with animals getting smarter
and people getting dumber
we may change roles some day

Where's Home?

Where do I belong
is there a place   for me?
We search and do not find
for we fail to see
home begins in the heart
and is found
where 'er we be.

Do I Believe?

I believe
except when I don't
when disappointment
comes my way
or fear rushes in
resentment covers the sun

I believe
but all too often
stumble and fall
with disbelief.

Ask for faith
when yours wanes
for protection
when you are afraid
for guidance
when you feel alone and lost.

Ask with the expectation
to receive what God
thinks is best for you
at this time.

Miracles

Let the miracles begin

in your life by allowing
them to come
noticing when they arrive
receive them in awe
overwhelmed in gratitude

Miracles are not rare
but they are God's glory
again and again they
reveal the power
of the Lord
watch for them
savor them
give thanks
and see them grow

Let the miracles begin
they've been here
all along
waiting for you
to receive the
love of the Lord

Breaking Chains

Kick the habit
break the chains
don't be a slave
to anything
set yourself free

We all have our

addictions
excesses
large or small
they may be
as long as we
have them
we can never
be truly free

Silent Conversations

Conversations with myself
what a bore I can be
whining, complaining
same old story again
and again

Why do we have this
constant negative chatter
in our heads and heart?
No wonder we can't read
each other's mind
we're doom be crazy, too
or die of boredom.

So how do we break this cycle
get excited about our lives
replace that black cloud
with sunny skies?

There's lots of techniques
but they seem to be

band=aids that
soon fall off.

The seed of discontent
cannot take root
in a grateful heart.

Resentment dissolves
with compassion
hate leaves
when the light
of love appears

Little-by-little
we become peaceful
sigh with serenity
grateful for life
with all its ups
and downs
in a world
that's not perfect
yet is filled with beauty
and opportunity
to live a rewarding life.

A Rushing Wind

Like a rushing wind
with a fire within
like a sleeping child
that knows no sin
life cycles there

and back again

Perhaps it's not people
who are "manic-depressive"
but rather life in general
ups and downs
highs and lows
peaks and valleys
choose your metaphor

Perhaps the secret
is to accept each day
for whatever it brings
riding out the storms
knowing soon there
will be sunny days.

Stepping Out of Life

I'm stepping out of life
watching it go by
occasionally taking
a deep breath
and jumping right in
then leaping out
when it's too much again

Party-Line Telephones

Party-line telephones

replaced by smartphones
cheese wrapped in
brown paper tied
with a string
now pre-sliced cheese
in a zip lock bag
covered dish suppers
kids playing kick-the-can
at sunset
mothers knitting by the fire
Dad close by

Now we have TV
and computer games
each one in his
make-believe world.
smartphone internet
replaces real conversation
in rockers on the porch
bushel basket of peas
to be shelled
love to be shared
on a summer afternoon.

Along the Way

I fly with
everlasting arms
beneath me
I use my fear
to fuel my courage
my faith in

the steadfastness of God
to continue
when I cannot see
the way.

The Lord is with me
each hour day-by-day.
His love sustains me
all along the way.

Begins With Me

Peace begins with me
first I must rid myself
of resentment
hairballs of fear
laziness has to go
love replaces all
this I've come to know

Rube's Cube

I cry for change
yet remain inflexible
serenity seems
illusive, temporary
always flitting away
perhaps it is an illusion
that peace, serenity, love
can stay

for it is an imperfect world
made with perfection
a conundrum
for mankind
who himself is perfection
with some flaws
a Rube's cube
full of possibilities
yet singular in solution

Polished to Perfection

A flower beneath
the iceberg grew
as beautiful as
the finest garden bloom

With grace does our
soul shine when
polished by duress
a diamond in the rough
brought to its innate perfection
with each cut bringing it
to Divine luster
for God's plan
is for each of us
to be what he
meant us to be
a rare gem shining with love
lighting the world
for others to see.

Find Your Joy

My life will end
somewhere, some day
it's been a good life
ups and downs along the way

One should not fear
that one's life has an end
but rather that we never
let it begin

Step forth with boldness
opportunities abound
make your life what
you want it to be
there's joy to be found

Not a Victim

I refuse to be a victim
choosing what I want
my life to be
I declare here and now
forever I'll be free

Freedom comes
from within, one can

find liberty in a prison cell
in pain and in confinement
amidst chaos can one
walk in serenity

God's grace fills me
with courage
His love shows the way
my life is what I make it
by my choices every day

Little or a Lot

Live a little
live a lot
live as if this life
is all that you've got

God Gave Me Life

I'd rather be alone
than with those who
pull me down.

I'd rather be
with those who
make me laugh
than one who
makes me cry.

I choose with care
who my friends will be
and do not
include some
who are my family.

The Lord gave me
my life but it is I
who choose how it
will be
I want a life filled
with love and light
and quiet serenity.

Free in a Prison

Free within, one can
find liberty in a prison cell
in pain and confinement
amidst chaos can one
walk in serenity

God's grace fills me
with courage
His love shows the way
my life is what I make it
by my choices each day.

Explosions

Explosion
dark energy moving outward
tainting all it touches
combining with like energy
causing waves to ripples
across the world
destroying all in its path

Anger breeds anger
when we respond
with a loving
compassionate heart
the light of love
neutralizes all darkness
for darkness can not
exist where there
is light

Apologies

For some, "I'm sorry"
is impossible to say
yet they show by
their actions
the apology unsaid

The same is true
about expressions
of love for we
each have our own way

to show we care

Let's allow these
differences of expression
accepting however
they're shared
for ultimately what's
important is the message
I care

Take Me

Take me
to heights unknown
show me
miracles divine

Dear, Lord
bless me, indeed
bathe me in
the grace of Your love
now and forever more

Sweet Mystery

My eyes now see
more than before
in layers revealed
of sweet mystery

My heart beats
in new rhythms of love
as I finally understand
how much
God loves me

Keeping Focused

Cultures have creation stories
how it all began
then there's speculation
on how it all will end

If it happened yesterday
I won't remember how
so I keep my focus
only on the now

Echoes

I'm living in echoes
reverberations across universes
going, going, going
then returning, returning, returning
the same but different
"The more things change
the more they remain the same."

Who am I
who are you

who are we?

Begin

Begin
continue
stop or go?
mazes of life
fix my path
twisting, turning
leading where
I do not know

Climbing

I climb
the mountain grows higher
I cry
tears cascade into waterfalls
I sing
silent songs that touch the stars

I am
or am I really?
Is there a me
or only a shadow
that has no home?
who am I
who are you
who are we?

Keep Focused

Maybe, possibly, probably
of course, we never know
what-ifs are useless
keep moving, we have to go

We cannot wait for answers
it seems they never come
so we walk our walk in faith
keep our focus
on the One.

Fruit

F lavors delicious, healthy, too
R ipened by the sun
U se from God's gardens
I mproves your health
T astes Divine and is

I walk through the floresta
sampling fruit along the way
fruit—God's gift to us
eat it every day

Some people don't have fruit
ever!
I am so blessed with abundant fruit

color wheels of delicious

Thank-you, God
for your gift of fruit.

Fall

Fall
golden leaves everywhere
failing to the ground
one remains
with a promise
of more to come
some warm spring day

I love fall
but wish
it could tiptoe past
winter's frigid days
to pussy willows of Spring
tulips along the way

Your Inner Being

Guard your inner being
that it be ever free
for darkness's grip is fast
only Light will guard you and me

Choose your words

gently, give no pain
speak not
let your anger wane

Guard your soul
that Light within
be careful who
you call your friend

More Than a Reservoir

Be not just a reservoir
of accumulated knowledge
rather become a fountain of wisdom
not a stagnant pool
of the thoughts of others
but rather a bountiful flowing river
of truth based on love

Unchanging Heart of Love

Our ideas can change
in one ear, out the other
our heads are not dependable
prejudice, fear, poor memory
murky waters make

But our hearts
filled with love
are as unchanging

as the tides

Let your actions and words
be guided by a pure heart
walk with the Lord by your side
His light is unchanging
through all eternity

The Dreamer

Be a dreamer
who makes his dreams
come true
for without our dreams
we float on
empty skies of blue.

At what age do
our dreams end?
When are we too old
to dream again?

Never, I tell you
for life is not over
until there's no more
breath to take
and our souls
go where 'er they go
to whatever dream we make.

How Many Truths?

How many things do I
know to be true
with absolute certainty?
Is truth so rare
that we're always
with a doubt?
Is there even
one thing of which
I have no question?
Indeed, there is:

There is a God
and He is Love.

All else can be unclear
for God's love
is full of light.

Give and Take

take
give
balance both

give receive
for both can be
blessed
yet without balance
either can do harm
for those who tend to give

learn to be a gracious receiver
and for you who always take
learn the sweet reward
of giving to others

Sound the Horn

Sound the horn
ring the bell
pay attention
to the tale
good guy, bad guy
how does the story end?

Perhaps it does not matter
for it's the journey
not the destination
on which the story
does depend.

Ice Cream

My dog likes ice cream
He licks the bowl with delight
Double dip again!

My God of Love

Is one book, one prayer
one religion, philosophy, doctrine
the right one, only one?
Are our social expectations
opinions, beliefs and motivations
the only acceptable ones
and all others are wrong
sinful, doomed?

Does the Creator pick
and choose groups of people
to "like" condemning all others
to eternal damnation?

I wonder if we paint god
in a model of our own frailties
vengeful, destroyer, wrathful?

And yet through all times
thought leaders speak
of a loving God

God of mercy
a forgiving father
who wants only for
His children
to be loving, too.

We each must decide
how we want to answer
the questions so often
pondered, debated.

The answer, I expect
can be found in our hearts
rather than our heads.

For me, my God is Love
only Love
who wants me to be
loving, too
sometimes not an easy
thing to do
but a lesson
I hope to master
with my Master
my God of Love.

Sacred Childhood

Let no one defile
the sacredness of childhood
that magical, innocent
time of wonder
the short period of life
when love is pure
and life delights

The Ugliness of Hypocrisy

Ah, the ugliness
of hypocrisy
arrogant struts

of judgmental slyness
liars pretending to be saints

Give me the man of humility
who admits his frailties
and forgives himself
and others
while striving to be
compassionate
loving to all

Was I Kind Today?

Was I kind today?
Did I stop to listen
help
soothe
care

K eep the divinity of kindness
I nsert a moment of love
N ever waste an opportunity to be kind
D evelop an attitude of kindness to all

Service

Being of service
blesses you and those you serve
there is a dignity in service
compassion

honor

To serve others in love
is noble and
its own reward

Be of Good Cheer

Cheerfulness
spreads
changes
dark to light

Be of good cheer
passing laughter
far and near
tucking smiles
along the way
spreading love
every day

On Fire

On Fire
I burn
there's no return
my heart's desire

Making pledges
promises to keep

going so deep
there's no return

Forgotten Promise

Silent shout
promise I forgot
good intention
had I

Disappointment
comes too soon
first the sun
then the moon

Days cycle in and out
good intention
had I
that somehow
never came to be

Is this how I
want my life to end
it's not too late
never too late
for life to start
again

Special Moments

Stuffed toy
lying on the rug
forgotten are
the moments of play
puppy asleep
lying at my feet
sweet way to end a day

Little moments
in the lifetime filled
with love
grateful am I
for a forgotten stuffed toy
and a puppy full of play

Fairy Tales

Green beans, fairy queens
Jack and Jill
went up the hill
fairy tales delight

More Than One

Give me back
my innocence
the time when I believed
good guys win
all's right in the end

Yet I am not bitter
haven't given up
on the possibility
that's there's much
I cannot see
perhaps even more
than one reality

The Art of Living Well

How does one live well
with silver forks
and golden goblets
finest schools
for the privileged few?

I walk the floresta
in early morn
water color hues
paint the streaks of clouds
stretching across the sky
a cacophony of birds
toss morning song
to each other across
the valley.

My life is peaceful
the frantic busyness
a past life is a bad
dream I left
breaking society's handcuffs

traded crowded shopping malls
for tranquil walks
by streams of sparkle

A good life consists
of taking each moment
as a gift…to be treasured
savored
lived to its upmost
regardless of wealth
or social position.

A good life
available to all
regardless of woe
for gratitude for each
blessing creates
a world to be treasured
gift from the creator
joy to each
who opens his heart
to receive.

Again

Again and again
history repeating
what does it take
for us to learn?

Why are we blind
unable to unwilling

to see
that war does not
make peace anger
cancels compassion
power is a quick
fading illusion.

The only stable truth
is that love
creates peace
calms anger
begets more love.

My Body

My body is a temple
created to contain
my soul divine.
Do I treat it as holy
or ignore its needs
disrespect its place
in a world created
by the Source of All?

All too often we do not
take good care of our bodies
expecting them to perform
in spite of neglect and abuse.
Today I will be grateful
for the miraculous body
God gave to me
treating it

with honor and care.

Priorities

Taking time
for what's important
priorities should be reviewed
too oft we fill our days
with busyness without
asking
How important is this
will it matter in a year from now
a week
tomorrow?

Darkness to Light

Large numbers of souls
leaving the earth
dooms day predictions
coming true
or cycles of life
creating, then fading?

Every generations
proclaims end of times
total destruction
of mankind
making us extinct
as the dinosaurs

of Earth itself
is predicted.
Can this happen?
Is its God's wrath
or man's greed
and indifference?

Yes, there are wrong
deeds done
changes to be made
but I refuse
to live in fear
and pessimism
choosing, instead
to live in gratitude
and the belief
that there is
evolution of man
in progress
which ultimately
turns darkness
to Light.

Ready?

Are you ready
to change your life
take charge
act instead of react?
How often we complain
yet do nothing
to change what we don't like.

We balm others
live our lives as a victim
wallow in self-pity.

If you don't like it
change it!
starting with yourself
what you cannot
change today
accept and move on

Serenity

Serenity is precious
unshakable
in the midst of chaos
it is the touchstone
to which we return
in times of crisis

Deep within comes
a knowing
that ultimately
all is well
life goes on
until it doesn't

S implify your life
E very day start with gratitude
R eact only with love
E ach one deserves to be honored
N ow is all we have

E ndless is God's love

See-Saw

People are complex
Never know what they will do
See-saw—Dark and Light

Mistakes

Mistakes—I've had a made a few
I expect that you have, too
Forgive mine if you will
As I forgive you and love you still

Comes and Goes

Fear comes and goes
even when our faith
is strong
remember this
and let it pass
with the certainty
that you are
loved and protected

Times of Crisis

In times of crisis
people rally
reaching out to help
those in need.
I believe in the innate
goodness of man
yet there are those
who seem consumed by evil.

Are their beings without souls
incapable of love and compassion?
The whole existence of evil
leaves much unanswered.
So I let it go

Who Am I?

Who am I to pen
poems of inspiration
every day
when all too often
I go astray?

My light sometimes flickers low
my faith often seems
to come and go

Having to learn my lessons
every day anew
will I ever learn them

thru and thru.

Lord, help this soul
who only want so love
like you.

Man of Greatness

We each become great
by the deeds that
we do that
are based decisions
guided by love.

Dare to be great
not by man's standards
rather in the measure
of the Lord.

Planting Dreams

Plant a dream
in the heart of someone young
a dream of excellence
whose light
will illuminate her path

A dream planted with care
is a gift divine
may each child have

someone who loves
enough to foster her dream.

Our Wisdom

Oh, that we have
the wisdom to trust
our hearts
the courage to follow
the tender light of faith.

May our mortal hearts
follow the whispers
of our souls divine
to live a life
of love through all time.

The Tap Root

May I be flexible
enough to bend
through storms of furry
rain and wind.

May the tap root of faith
keep me strong
knowing that never
am I alone.

Our Wisdom

Oh, that we have
the wisdom to trust
our hearts
the courage to follow
the tender light of Earth.

May our mortal hearts
follow the whispers
of our souls divine
to live a life
of love through all time.

Nothing's Impossible

I laugh at
impossibilities
make them my goal
dream the impossible dream
for if we do only
what we think we can
we become mired in the mundane

Think big, then bigger
over the top, out of the box
try the outrageous
even the thing you most fear
stretch your mind and soul
to the stars
and into the Great Beyond
for only then will you begin to be

all that you
are meant to be

Pioneer of Faith

Become a pioneer of faith
much greater than a mustard seed
go where only dreamers go
knowing with unbridled faith
that you will never go
so far that
God is not with you

God's Plan

Does God have a plan?
all of nature is made
with such precision
Golden Mean, Fibonacci sequences
patterns in nature
including our bodies
cycles of life
stars, moon, tides
Does God have a plan?

Who am I to ask "why?"
when something seems wrong
how dare I rail
and rant at life's woes
for all that I experience

contains a lesson
if I am willing to learn
a part of God's plan
even if I don't yet understand

Are evil deeds, natural disasters
suffering children
part of God's plan
I do not know
so go with what
I believe to be
true to me:
God is love
He loves me
guides me
has a plan for me
that I willingly
follow to the end of time
and into the Great Beyond

Faith Grows

If faith does not grow
unbelief edges in
the more we trust
that inner voice
the stronger it grows

Be still, listen
discern its guidance
from your desires
surrender and follow

even when you
cannot understand
ask for clarity
faith and courage
to follow the Divine voice
that guides us from within.

No Need to Shout

I need not shout
for elegance is found
in stately trees
hushed starlit night
of quiet beauty
that leaves one in awe

My power comes from within
never do I demand
for he who responds
to the energy Divine
also has this knowing
binding us as one
to One through all time.

Wait

Sit quietly do I and wait
no more rushing here and there
I wait with joy and serenity
knowing, open, ready to receive

the voice of love
guiding me

I Believe

I believe except when I don't
then once again I ask for faith
which comes as sure as
sun and rain
then I believe once again

The Mark

Mark of the Beast
signs of Satan
sin, sin, sin
must mankind be
controlled by fear?
Are we at the end
of times where
damnation lurks

War, economic collapse
natural disasters
across the globe

CLICK

No more "news"
turn off fear

my God is a God of Love
only Love
eternal Love
unconditional Love

He does not destroy
my enemies or yours either
no vengeance
eternal damnation

God is love
an He wants me
to love, too
the same is true
for you
just this.

Value of Prayer

What is the value of prayer?
Does it cause God to
help one family
but not another
change course of events
in natural disaster
does it stop killing, crime
corruption?

Why do we pray?
We pray to draw closer
to the Divine
understand we're not alone

nor invincible
we pray to booster faith
to express our soul's deepest yearnings
to find peace
in our God of love.

Who Is My Judge?

How easily you enumerate
my perceived faults
yet seldom do I hear
my virtues.
Can it be that I'm
so bad that there
are not to see?

Yet others tell me
otherwise wo who am I
to believe?

Neither, I expect
for only God will
be my judge
my God of mercy
compassion, patience
pure Love

Neither you nor I
can be such fair judges
so to him do I turn
to know who I am
He calls me Beloved

it's good enough for me.

Storms of Anger

Be silent
let the storms of anger
pass
do not fan the flame
rather let it die
with no fuel added
silence
a peaceful heart

and knowing someone's
anger says more about them
than you
be at peace
willow in a storm
compassionate, patient, silence
is the best reply

He Is Happy

Happy is he
who is content
with what life brings
lessons offered
receiving with good heart

Peaceful is he

who is grateful
for all, finding
treasures everywhere
savoring each in its time

Within Infinity

I go within
free from the pull
of a world of chaos
deep, deeper
into the kernel
of peace
spark of light

I am home
expanding into
the Great Beyond
leaving universes
I enter the Divine
Source of All
I am home
at peace

I am where
nothing of this world
can touch me
for I merge
into the Light
into infinity

Higher and Higher

Climbing
higher and higher
out of the mire
of the world of woe

Mountain top view
of the beauty of the Earth
reminds me that our Creator
created a world of beauty
and it is we who
disturb its balance

Will our children live
in a world of beauty
of peace, compassionate love?
Or will they live
in the chaos and destruction
we are creating each day?

Dear Lord, help us to see
with us lies
the fate of humanity.

Angels Sing

Wonder if it's true
the angels sing in the sky
yes, if you listen

Peter Pan Puppy

>Think I'll be
>a Peter Pan puppy
>always ready to play
>snuggle, give wet kisses
>sleeping in the sun all day

Hour Before Dawn

>The hour before dawn
>air fresh, sky beginning to lighten
>day full of possibility
>I sit quietly, pen in hand
>writing what comes to me
>every day without fail.
>This is where I'm meant to be.
>
>Do you start your day
>in quiet reflection
>open your heart to receive
>fortify your faith through prayer?
>
>This time at the beginning
>of each day made sacred
>by observance
>can set the tone
>for the rest of your day
>to hear God's guidance
>all along the way.

My Duty?

Do I have a duty?
To what? to whom?
Who decides what my duty is
what I can and cannot do?

Follow the rules
obey the laws
salute the flag
observe the holidays
rituals, doctrines

Have I ever made
a conscious decision
about where I want
to commit my loyalty
obedience or am I swept
along the floods of demand?

Obedience is not commitment
fear of consequences is not loyalty
I choose to serve our Creator

to follow His direction to
always act with love
to do no harm
love one another
any dictate that tells me
I must act otherwise
is not my duty.

Not the Wisest

I'm not the wisest
or the most knowledgeable
but I do have a mind
capable of thought
a heart that can discern
will to choose
responsibility for my choices.

It is never someone else's fault
for each choice
has led me where
I am today.

I stand on firm ground
learn from my mistakes
forgive myself and others
try to do better in the future.

I am human
with frailties and faults
but also with the capacity
to love without bounds
under the compassionate
guidance of our Creator.
This is all I need to be.

Only Me

Daddy's pretty little girl
mirror, mirror on the wall

am I the fairest of them all?

Daddy's brave little man
don't cry, sissies cry
play football, only
fags are artists

I love being an old woman
no girdles of my youth
obsession with my weight
eyeliner, lipstick, perms for me
for I declare I am free
to be exactly as time
has made me be
an old woman
who does not want
to be anything
but me.

Old

O nly the body ages
L ove that my spirit stays young
D on't have to be an old fogy

Free?

I
am
not

free
if
I
am
afraid

Faith
turns
fear
into
trust
in
He
Who
Is
All

Bitter on the Tongue

It's taste is bitter
on the tongue
oh, how we love to criticize
next time
substitute something
you like about the person

Old-Fashioned Virtues

Stand together
loyalty and commitment

are still virtues to honor
just be sure they are for
a worthy cause

White Lies

I'm always truthful
Except when I tell white lies
White lies are still lies!

Pretty Poems

Pretty poems
rousing rants
declaring discussions
worthy words
nothing nonsense

Sometime the best poem
is an empty space.

Are You Kind?

Let all acts
start with kindness.
How Kind am I
are you?

K eep respect in your voice and heart
I nsist that all be treated with kindness
N ever pass an opportunity to be kind
D o acts of kindness every day

Who Started It?

She started it
it's her fault
regardless of another's behavior
how we respond
is our choice

A loving response
is always better
than to act in kind

Simply Simple

S top extravagance, live simply
I nvite serenity into your life
M ore is not better, use gratitude instead
P eople can save the Earth. Do your part.
L ove works under all circumstances
E ach act is a choice

So Busy

I live in a culture
that glorifies busyness
where being idle is a fault
multi-tasking is an illusion
of productiveness
more is better
relaxation comes in a pill
or drink

I feel guilty
lying in a hammock
reading a book
surely that can't be right

I want to learn
not only the art
of doing nothing
but how to say
that's what I'm doing
without guilt

Goodbye to Gloom

Goodbye to gloom
and doom
yes, there's plenty of
bad left to see
but daisies and humming birds
are where I choose
each day my focus to be

Woven in Woe

Life can be completed
tribulations woven in a matt
woes of this or that
yet
life can be sweetly simple
when we lay our burdens down
at the feet of our Lord
in Him is serenity found

When?

When is enough, enough?
when I stop coming back for more
when I make my boundaries clear
when I finally say Enough
and say it loud enough to hear!

Bubble Dreams

Bubble of beauty
Floating upward to the sky
Please don't burst my dream

Next Morning Regrets

Next morning regrets
I've had a few
be willing to be
you've had them, too

Wonder why I never learn
if I do it
I'm gonna' get burned

Thinking

Thinking, always thinking
worry about this
crabbing about that
problem is I never stop to see
all the blessings
God has given me

Gonna' change my ways
cancel thoughts so dark
go within to find that spark
gonna' stand in the Light
let it shine
fill my heart with gratitude
let loving thoughts
fill my mind.

My Anchor

You are my anchor
on troubled sea
a rock upon which
I stand
all that comes
You'll guide me through
my life is in Your hand

Sea Breezes

Cloudless sky so hot
Waves beckon us to the beach
Sea breezes refresh

So Rare

Skin—peaches and cream
She blushes so easily
Charm and innocence

So rare these days

Walking to Nowhere

Sidewalk leading nowhere
walking with determination

don't know where I'm going
but I better hurry
so I rush through my days
never knowing where I've been

Doing God's Will

I walk with steps firm
no backward glances
reluctant tread
mixed feelings
including a sense of dread

There is a light
spread around me
as I do God's will
as if it were my own
which it is

My heart beats
with serenity
my breath is filled with joy
God's almighty strength
unending love
is all I need forever more

Elastic Dreams

Elastic are my dreams
stretching here with hope

there with fear
back to center with faith

Tear drops fall from
storm darkened clouds
yet a lustrous rainbow
caps the sky
proclaiming God's grace
forever more

Loveliness of Faith

Oh the loveliness of faith
the Light that banishes darkness
dries tears, fills us with hope
unseen though it may be
faith through eternity

Opinions!

O pinions—I've had a few
P ractically all were biased
I gnoring other possibilities
N ever far from self-serving
I nviting only who agree with me
O pen to other ideas is rare
N oth considering all sides
S eems like I need to quit having

Opinions!

Just Laugh

Sometimes I just laugh
At the world's absurdities
Nothing else will do!

Great

Know that you are great
divine in conception and execution
love with greatness
hatred dissolved
cling to nothing
not in harmony
with universal good.

Listen to the wise silent voices
shutting out the cacophony
of misdirection
know that spiritual laws
always supersede the material

Claim your joy
in knowing you are
part of the web of Light
across eternity

Dance of Ribbons

Dance of the ribbons
looping rainbows
lovely ladies
swooping, bending swaying
park surprise, what a delight!

Today's Laugh

Did I laugh today
deep down belly laugh
knee slapping, can't stop laugh
a laugh that makes everyone else
laugh, too?

If not, shame on me
shame on you, too
for wasting a day
gotta' leave time to play

Body Drumming

Clap my hands
clap yours, too
pick-up the beat with my shoe
snap of the fingers
sounds so neat
different parts of our body
pick up the beat

Car Games

Games in the car
when you gotta' go far
keeps parents sane
kids don't fight
if you know lots of games

Morning Mantras

Time to go
where's my shoe
nowhere to be found
what should I do
if I don't hurry up
I'll be late for school

Morning mantra
repeated each day
you'd think we'd find
a better way!

Sneaky Cat

Cat burst her bubble
gum everywhere
he snickers,

slides away
swishes his tail
without care

No Easy Way

There is no easy way
no short cuts in life
gotta' keep on going
just trusting in the Lord
both night and day

Tickets for the lottery
slick deals, climb
the ladder in the backs
of other, going to get
to the top, no matter what.

There's no short cuts in life
doesn't matter what you've got
if you don't have the Lord
doesn't matter what you've bought

Mistletoe Kiss

Under mistletoe waiting for a kiss
Finally he comes to kiss me
It's mistletoe bliss

Lean on Me

Lean on me
says the Lord
when you are weary
afraid to go on
lean on me
for together
you are strong

We often whine and pray
give me this, or that, we say
but how often do we sit
open to receive
surrendering our will
finally ready
to follow God's advice
lean on me for together
you are strong

In the Silence of Prayer

I live within
the silence of prayer
'tis a quiet valley
where I can be with God
undisturbed by the
chaos of mankind

This holy place of prayer
is always with me
comforting, guiding

healing all sorrow
a sanctuary I may go to
where I can be
in silent connection
with the Divine
Light of the Lord

Hidden Fire

There burns a hidden fire
my soul's connection
to the mystical light
which cleanses, purifies
readies me to receive

I sit in readiness
heart open to receive
the love energy
of the Lord

Reverence

Reverence seems lost
churches that look like
rock star settings
strobe lights, dancing girls
in tight clothes

What happened to quiet prayer
reassuring icons of yesteryear

awe of God
who needs no snare drums
just humble reverence
and a willingness to
receive the grace of God

Taking

Taking
without giving
is stealing in the end

More

Acquisition
buy, get, take
mountains of more
will never replace love
for he who has no love
is a pauper forever more

Pretty Poems

Pretty poems
rousing rants
declaring discussions
worthy words
nothing nonsense

Sometimes the best poem
is an empty page

Walking in Faith

Faith is the queen of virture
false proof we accept as truth
sometimes we just have to let go
and walk in faith
that sweet knowing
that God is by our side
now and forever more.

The Perfect Life

Suppose life was what
you wanted it to be
perfect in every way
day after day of pleasure
how long would it take
before you felt bored?
Then what would you do?

Summer Fun

Lick the popsicle
fast before it melts away

happy summer fun

Mirror's Truth

The mirror of the world
shows me my face
when I am glum
only dark clouds
do I see

Ah, but when my heart
is at peace
the reflection
is a sweet summer day
filled with flowers
butterflies and skies
so blue the angels sing

Leave Room for Faith

Do not explain away
the mysteries of the divine
with sage philosophies
rigid religions
cultural expectations

Leave room for the
unfathomable
awe
humility

faith

When I Want to Quit

Sometimes I give up
quit, don't want to
do this anymore
too hard, God
this life You gave me
can't do it anymore

My child, He whispers
I will help you
never do I leave you alone

Hearing these words
lifts the burden
lightens the load
renews my faith
and I continue on
renewed, knowing
God is ever with me
helping me each
step of the way

Backslider

How quickly I slide
back down the mountain
how slowly I climb up again

Wish it was the
other way around

Call in the Clowns

Call in the clowns
fill the balloons
let's have a party
get rid of the gloom

Tell everyone
come and play
by hook or crook
it's a happy day

I grumble as I get out of be
knees ache, gonna' rain
whine about this
complain about that
what a way to
start my day

Then I decide
which I want
bring in the clowns
it's a happy day

A Rose

Am I a rose
or a simply daisy
perhaps a rare
boom at night
morning glory
that opens in early light

I am all flowers
rainbows, too
hummingbirds
mountain dew

I'm part of all
the beauty
God makes each day
He's right beside me
come what may

Courtesy

Always be polite
regardless of who is right
courtesy helps all

Pearls of Grace

Strands filled with

pearls of grace
received one by one
my necklace grows full
with God's generosity

Call in the Clowns

Call in the clowns
fill the balloons
let's have a party
get rid of gloom
tell everyone
come and play
by hook or crook
it's a happy day!

I grumble as I
get out of bed
knees ache, gonna' rain
whine about this
complain about that
what a day to
start my day.

Then I decide
which I want
bring in the clowns
it's a happy day!

Love Is A Verb

Love is a verb
never a noun
do it
don't just talk
about it!

Meek and Humble

Meek, humble
seldom do some
strive to be
aggressive, ambitious
go-getters admired
fame, wealth desired

sports stars, divas
rock legends
industry giants
Montesano
pharmaceutical companies
getting rich on our suffering

Let's examine our values
our actions tell our beliefs
is there value in being
meek, humble
compassionate
respectful, loving?

Guilty I Am

I'm the first to raise my hand
guilty am I and all of you
but of what
seems like everything
what would the world
be like without guilt?

Who established the rules
by which we live
have we ever stopped
to consider if these
should be our values

G et free of guilt
U se common sense
I nvestigate your values
L ove based actions work
T ake charge of who you are

Time to Stop

Plodding along
one step, one step
gonna' get there
wherever "there" is

Racing around
always running
multi-tasking, striving
hurrying to get there

wherever "there" is

Where are we going?
Where do we want to be?
Are we living the life
we want?
Are we living the life
God wants us to live?

I stop
really stop
go within
ask, wait to receive
to hear that inner guidance
we all have
if only we stop
really stop
and go within

Getting Stronger

A muscle gets stronger
if you use it
so does faith
sometimes we just
have to step off
step out
trusting that
all is well
whatever happens
opens doors of opportunity
to discover who

we have always been
a child of God
with a core of Divine
totally separate
from this material world
where we err, stumble, fall

Oh, Lord, please help me
make my faith stronger
give me opportunities
to use and build it
courage and strength
to step out and trust

F ull belief
A fraid no more
I n God do we trust
T hankful for each grace
H eart-centered in all we do

A Thing of Beauty

A thing of beauty
marvelous to behold
great art, music
sunsets, night skies
aglow
a tiny daisy
picked by a child
made marvelous to behold
as she give it to me with love

A Passing Glance

A passing glance
not a stare
hardly noticed
and yet
it remains with me
her smile as she passed by

Sometimes we give and receive
simple blessings
that light our way
be sure and give someone
a smile today

Half-a-Health Nut

Some exercise
others do not
some brush their teeth
while others let them rot

I'm half-a-health nut
go exercise then stop
for ice cream
what can I say?

At Least I Try

Better if I try
I can't do it if I don't
Wow, look, I did it!

Weary Am I

I have grown weary of voices
that never seem to dim
my heart grows heavy
with battles I can't win

So many places
I want to go no more
where fields of darkness do lie
where flowers grew before
now they simply die

Is there no place
where I can find
the mountain of prayer
with a sweet voice call
"Come, be Mine"

I weep and seek
this love so true
'til finally I hear
come, come, my child
I'll comfort you

Reflections

Reflections do not always
speak the truth
fun house mirrors
trees on lake's edge
reflect upside down

Mirror on the wall
who is this woman I see
troubled heart, hair so grey
can this crone be me?

Then suddenly there is
an amazing transformation
before my eyes a revelation
my smile brings light
from deep within
that sacred place
that's always been

Wonder

W e seek to comprehend
O ur universe fills us with awe
N ever do miracles cease
D arkness melts away
E ver the shadow are we
R ealizing we need the light

Sunset Reflections

butterfly wings aflame
sunset casts its golden glow
whose evening sheen
mimics the colors of the sky
each evening I come
to lay down the burdens
of the day
in exchange
of peace God gives us
each night as we stop
to say
thank you

Worry Free

I fear what might happen
like rocks piled high
those worries reach the sky
yet here I am
safe and sound
none of those worries
to be found

Silly me
when will I learn
to let those worries flee
to trust God is with me
ready to set me free

Mystery

It is the mystery
from which worship blooms
our awe that brings forth
the need to connect
with the Divine
the tiny speck of Light within
expanding into eternity

M ystical is He who seeks
Y ield to the voice within
S ee God's glory in all
T ake time each day to receive
E very soul is Divine
R eality starts within
Y our truth comes from inside

Thus Divine

A baby, a leaf, tiny grain of sand
an immensity, a world
piece of creation
thus Divine

Expectation

Expect death
for its certain to come
be grateful instead

for the time you have

Expect life to have
its ups and downs
both offering opportunity

Expect mystery, awe
joy, tears, laughter
as we experienced all
life brings
for our expectation
lightens the load
preparing us with the knowing
that with time
all shall pass
waves bring tides
which come and go
in cosmic ways of mystery

Forgotten Shoe

Shoe by the side of the road
I pause to wonder
who left it there
was there an accident
and its owner no longer
needs a pair?

I leave a trail
wherever I go
parts of me
I no longer

need or want
lay down sorrow
discord resentment
do away with fear
I want to rid myself
of all that weighs me down
until my steps are light
and I'm finally free.

Allowing Life's Mysteries

Should we stop speculating
quit asking "why"
let life unfold
in its certain and uncertain ways?

Why must we explain everything
thus tarnishing the beauty
of mystery
deleting our faith
spoiling God's surprise?

Rather let's live in
happy expectation
in awe of all
we experience
in faith that we
are part of God's mystery
and content to be just that.

The Void

> Oh, the longing of my heart
> neither diamonds or gold
> can satisfy the immortal soul
> indeed, only He who made us
> can fill this void
> and He does as soon
> as we allow Him
> into our hearts and life

The Immensity of God

> God's immensity is measured
> in numberless stars
> droplets of water
> in bottomless seas
> time without beginning or end
> unending love for
> all He has created
> until the end of eternity.

The Flower

F orever cycles of beauty
L ovely reminders of God's grace
O ne day without flowers is too many
W e remember the Earth's beauty in flowers
E ach flower is a token of God's love
R ejoice in God's gift of flowers

All to Come

I do not wish to see
the failings of men
nor hear their unkind words
Lord, make me blind and deaf
and if my tongue speaks ill
take it, too
for I want only to
be just like You.

Let me be like gentle breezes
sweet cheeps of baby birds
soft putters of rain drops
silent as morning fogs
rolling across verdant valleys

Surround me, fill me
with Your love
make me worthy
of the beauty
of this world
and all to come.

Lost God

To he who is lost
God is, too

yet God is everywhere
part of all you see
and do not see

Breath deeply
for even in the air
God is there

Feel the warmth of the sun
let its light fill your soul
for God is the sun
part of all He creates
heavens, earth, and sea
yes, even you and me

At Last at Peace

Let me lose the woes and wails
in fields of clover
tides of the sea
billowing clouds
rustling of trees
humming bees

I give my soul
the gift of walking
along trails on mountains high
singing old tunes
of the sweet by-and-by
letting all cares slip away

At last at peace

I lay my head
on boughs of green
to sleep a sleep
of harmony
in the forest of love
there but unseen

Worry Free

I fear what might happen
like rocks piled high
those worries reach to the sky
yet here I am
safe and sound
none of those worries
to be found

Silly me
when will I learn
to let those worries flee
to trust God is with me
ready to set me
now and forever free

Piano

P laying lifts my soul
I play away sorrows
A m at peace when I finish
N ever fails to give me joy

O h, Lord, thank-you for music

Last Chance

Deserts where
majestic cedars once reined
sun, heat, withered life
our march of destruction
moves on

What creature
would destroy his lair
pollute water he needs to drink
create fogs of death
from air he needs to breathe

I know of none but man

M an is abusing the gift of life
A lways war, greed and power
N ow is our last chance to change

Sprigs of Joy

I pick off specks of pettiness
rub away stains of greed, jealousy
rancor, cleanse away spite
until I wear a raiment
pure enough to let the light
of love, compassion, generosity

shine through

I wear this cloak
with sprigs of joy
wreaths of smiles
a dash of fun,
lots of good humor
attired for the Ball of Life
grateful for He who guides me
through darkness and into
the light where my soul
was destined to go

Tongueless Silence

Let us claim
the tongueless silence
vow never to speak again
rather than ever say
an unkind word
that cuts the heart
of another

Be silent
dissolve your criticism
anger, jealousy
with an outpouring of love
until no longer
are your words a weapon
but rather a light
that shines on the world
too often in woe

The Race Is On

Let's have a race
where all form a horizontal
line which is maintained
to the finish line

Should anyone lag behind
those nearby give a helping hand
while the rest slow down
to help them catch up

Let's have a life
where the race is not over
until all pass the Pearly Gates
where we help each other
along the way
so everyone wins
champions are all
of the game of life
where we're sent
to learn how to love

A Tiny Hand

Her tiny hand
sweetly took mine
as we walked
along the way

meadow flowers, drifting clouds
birds of plumage fine
become even more lovely
when she slipped her hand
in mine

There is an innocent trust
in this little girl
that I had so long ago
Dear lord, may I put
my hand in yours
to once again know
this glow

Angel of Prayer

Oh, angel of prayer
please guide this restless soul
teach me how to pray
not lists of wants
nor whiney complaints
rather words of praise
gratitude and love

May my prayers be songs
to honor my God
who is so generous to me
may I kneel in awe
vow my love now
and until eternity

What Money Can't Buy

Joy cannot be bought
nor can serenity
trust only comes
from the grace of God
who fills the hearts
of those who love
and live in harmony

Life's Sweetness

Do not gather gall
when sweetness surrounds you
keep your focus on the
nectar of flowers
bees gathering
transforming into honey

Listen to the sweetness
of birds singing their
morning songs
daintiness of dew drops
clinging to fairy webs

The shear delight of the world
in its generous beauty
delights if one
is willing to see

Last Leaf

Last leaf of autumn
Please hold on tight for awhile
Keep the snow away

Lips

L ift our voices in praise
I nvite God into your heart
P raise to remind us of God's greatness
S tart your days with praise and gratitude

How to Be

How many ways to be grateful
loving, compassionate, kind
count the stars, grains of sand
blades of grass sprinkled with dew
let the number grow and grow
and never will you reach the end
of love, a force of infinite power

Lord, teach me how to love as You do
show me how to be ever
grateful
compassionate
kind
even until the end of forever

Battle of the Bulge

Pancakes piled high
slathered in butter
and maple syrup
side order of crisp bacon

May I please have an order
of fat-free yogurt sprinkled
with low calorie granola

Next life I want
a perpetually thin body!

Too Old to Learn

Too old to learn
or do this or than
self-imposed limits
learned from a culture
that youth
and shuts old people
away in senior citizens
centers, nursing homes
housing where only old people live

Let me dance with the young
tell stories filled with
laughter and wisdom

learn new things
on YouTube and classes
shared by all ages

Let me be part of society
part of the family
be patient when my steps
are slow, my hearing dim
when I repeat a story
again and again
for within this aging body
is a souls who stays young
who wants your acceptance
and love to the very end

Running in Circles

Running in circles
never getting anywhere
life on a treadmill
without hope

"Nothing changes
if nothing changes"

Breaking the cycle
trying something new
climbing out of my rut
it's been long overdue

No Friend

Climbing up the mountain
sliding down again
know I could make it
if only I had a friend

So, you may ask
why do you have no friend?
it's a question worth pondering
for the answer's always within

Take a Bow

Sometimes I'm so mature
but then I'm often not
I try my best to get it right
give it all I got

I screwed-up, I admit it
not rare at all
I'm not yet perfect
so sometimes I take a fall

I'm learning to accept
how I am right now
forgive myself when I need to
and when I get it right
to take a bow

Making a List

Making a list now
to help me not forget stuff
where'd I put my list?

Skipping Still

I no longer skip
Nor do I kneel for prayer
And my mirror lies

No More Gossip

I'd tell you a secret
but I can't remember it
God's laughing
at a has-been gossip

Not Going to Hell

Going to be good now
don't want to go to hell
heard they had a dentist there
that gives you a tooth implant
every day—making a saint
out of me!

Sea Horse Magic

I dove into the ocean
a sea horse greeted me
I climbed aboard, off we went
I'm as happy as I can be

A mermaid met us
a secret she did say
flipped her tail
swam away singing
have a happy day

All around the ocean
we swam, my trusty
steed and I
'twas but a dream
that I'll remember
until the day I die.

Sunrise Miracle

Once upon a miracle
the sunrise I did find
it's splendor never repeated
it's always one of a kind

Truth-telling

The bell rings when
a truth is told
but it's been a long time
since we heard it ring

Are there no more truths
to tell
is everything just a lie
have people forgotten honesty
a value that did die

I'm going to tell the truth today
if just for this one day
to demonstrate to myself and all
truth telling's a better way

Knight of Good Deeds

Knight in shining armor
riding his valiant steed
trying to find something to do
that counts as his daily good deed

What if everyone did
a good deed each day
would we use up all the good deeds
or are there more along the way

Look around my friends
find something to do

to help someone
lift a burden they have
help them to start anew

Remembering God

How long has it been
since you thought of God
did you stop
throughout your day
to thank the Lord
for all the gifts
He's strewn along the way

Did you feel the cool breeze
hear the birds deep in song
did you feel God's love
reassuring you
He's there
you're never alone

Despair

D ooms day thoughts
E very day tears flow
S eems like woe will never end
P ots of gold empty, rainbows fade away
A ll hope is lost
I finally remember "this, too, shall pass"

Punish?

Do we need to punish
to correct a wrong?
Is there no other way?
What would the world be like
if we used love
to teach and guide.
each one
It would be a better world, I'd say.

Country Fair

Off to the country fair
there's rides and exhibits there
cotton candy, hot dogs to eat
house of mirrors, can't be beat

Haven't been in a very long time
if I stay off the rides, I'll be just fine
never too old to enjoy the fair
hope to see all of you there

Making a House a Home

Make your house your home
add pictures and items you like

let it be your haven
a place of peace where
you can relax and feel safe

Add God's presence to your home
invite Him to stay
add candles, delicious country smells
songs you love to sing
always keep it nice and clean
make your house a sacred home

Candles in the Windows

Lights to come home to
candles in the front windows
tradition of love

Alchemy of Error

Dear Lord, help me be kind today
if I am not
help me learn from my mistakes
may I be free of envy and judgment
if I fail this, too
help me to see a more loving
way to be
may all my faults and mistakes
become lessons of humility
gratitude, compassion
and love

Too Neat

Why am I so neat
everything in its place
clean 'til it sparkles?
when does a virtue
turn to an annoyance?

Shower Songs

Sing in the shower
Great way to start out our day
Have a happy day!

Diet, Rule #1

Here's the dieting rule
If I like it, can't eat it
Exception—pizza

Working Hard

Live to love
what if you were paid
to be loving

that was your job
would you be rich
or a beggar on the street?

No Bad News

Turn off the news
hurricane reports
any drama in your life
let it go
shutting all negative
happening, instead
focusing on the good
things all around us
every day
God's gifts, grace, love

Pass out the blessing
of your smile
that lights someone's day
be a beacon of love

Take Control of Your Life

Strike a match--it's hot
Add some ice to make it cold
Take control of life

Don't Help a Fool

You cannot make
a fool wise
he who is ready to change
will of his own accord.

Be careful who you help
the world is full of takers
stealing from those in true need.

All need compassion
but do not take away
a much needed lesson.

Don't Hold on to Envy

How tightly we hold
on to envy and jealously
rendering us incapable
of true gratitude
for the daily blessings
we receive.

The Inconvenience of Poverty

Poverty is no disgrace
but it is very inconvenient
yet even the poor
can enjoy summer showers

harvest moons
and a sunrise
that turns the sky
to joyous colors
of sweet design.

Self-Love

You love me more
that I know how to
love myself
criticizing my body
You gave me
everything I do seems
not good enough.
I fall into the pit
of hopelessness so easily.

Lord, teach me how to
love, starting with myself
for how can I love others
when I can't love myself?

Steadfastness of the Lord

The steadfastness
of the Lord is sure.
Renew your faith
in His love every day.

Act with faith
that you are being guided
every step of the way
if you have given your
obedience to the Lord.

Weed to Flower

The weed becomes a flower
the moment you want it.
Love someone
and they, too, will blossom
in God's garden of life.

My Wealth

Little money do I have
yet I am rich
for wealth is not
measured in coin
but rather in recognizing
God's blessing freely given
to us each day.

Pleasing People

Pleasing people
is a waste of time

so quickly do they forget
but pleasing God
takes you into
an eternity of love.

The Holiness of Prayer

Pray not with eloquence
but rather with earnestness.
Prayer is meant to elevate the soul
toward its Master.
Prayer guides us to understanding
the infinite holiness of He
to whom we lift our hearts in prayer.

God is always ready to hear
to help, to bring peace to our soul.
Prayer is a powerful means
of resisting sin
and advancing holiness.

P eace is found through prayer
R ejoice knowing God hears our prayers
A nger dissolves through prayer
Y our prayers open the door of love
E ach prayer is a light along your path
R enew your faith through prayer

Planting a Seed

Seeds in a pod
grow differently
some are straight and tall
others grow crookedly

Our children also grow
differently
some due to innate qualities
others the push and pull
of family and cultural demands

Plant your seeds well
it's the most you can do
what fruits they bear
depends on more than you

Grandmother's Table

So much love was there
Grandmother's kitchen table
Pie served with laughter

Summer Treat

Picking strawberries
One for him, one saved to sell
Basket—slow to fill

Wait to Marry

Don't marry too young
Wait 'til you are old enough
To know what love is

Old Age

Everyone gets old
It's an important life phase
A time to reflect

Creaky Yoga

Stretch, bend, then you twist
Body making old age sounds
Yoga for seniors

Bathroom Library

Sitting on the throne
Reading a book in the bathroom
Stealing time for me

Morning Laugh

Fun inspiration
A poem to make you laugh
Gift to start your day

Never Late

Never am I late
My life is well organized
Punctuality

Thy Will

"…Thy will be done…"
What does it mean
to do God's will
rather than our own?

Does it mean we can
never do anything we
want to do? No,
rather we must learn
to align our desires
with God's will
to give cheerful obedience
surrender with joy
to have such love
in our hearts that
we act with honor

toward God and
all He created.
Only then can
we truthfully pray:

"Thy will be done!"

Sour Puss

Sour pickles—yum
A sour puss is not fun
Switch to sweet pickles

Dreams of My Heart

Bring sweet dreams to my eyes
enter the open door
of my heart
and stay forever
for I am Yours
now and forever more.

Your Presence

Your presence is as subtle
as a flower not yet
in blossom
yet I feel You

hear You, know You are near.

You come with my tear drops
whispering words of love
singing my name again and again.
You are with me to eternity.

Won't Try

Ask the sun to leave
impossible
ask the clouds to not rain
when the fields are dry
ask me to stop loving You
I won't even try

Surround and Within

Soft as candlelight
whisper of wind
You surround me
and go within

Becoming You

I want to see You
to feel the power
to know Your glory

I want to feel You
to know You
to become You
merge, transform
to become part of
Your glow

Parade

Follow the parade
I don't know where we're going
good time 'til we're there

It's time
to fly
everyone
persevere

Time to fly
lift your wings
open your heart
receive the Light
Fly to the Great Beyond

Not the Same

Cherry filled chocolates
A sweet childhood memory
Low fat yogurt now

Kind Flowers

Loving words scattered
like flowers in a meadow
healing wounded hearts

Unmeasurable

How do you measure
a sunbeam
mother's devotion
a baby's trust?

Some things just are
and are meant to be
no explanation needed
such as faith
an unmeasurable gift
of God's grace.

Life's Rut

Stuck in life's deep rut
open your heart to God's love
your life will blossom

Teenage Lament

I want to be
like other people
one of the crowd
just the same
yet I am uniquely me
just trying to learn
the acceptance fame

She spends hours
in front of her mirror
painting a face that's
just the same
clothes rejected
are scattered everywhere
not good enough
to play the game

The best part of growing older
is when I learned how
to play the game
then realized I did not have to
and quit trying
to be the same

Now I'm me
and that's just fine
aging well
like a good bottle of wine

Watch Your Language

Language--chaste and sincere
a rare commodity
use most those words
that elevate, teach, love

Words of Truth

Sweet words of truth
spoken in love
inspired by the Divine
is a gift indeed.

A Healthy Tongue

If the doctor
examines your tongue
to determine your physical health
we would do well to
do the same to know
the status of our
spiritual health

A silent tongue
guards peace
a kind tongue reassures
tongues filled with gratitude
open hearts
and brings light to the soul

Roller Coaster Ride

Living with a teenager
is a roller coaster ride from hell
drama is the byword
even when things are going well

Up, then down
round and round we go
thank-God I'm old
and off this ride
I'm chilling out
taking life slow

Live

Live
not just exist
waiting for death
wallowing in self-pity

Live
each precious moment
help others
to know the wonder
of life

What Might Have Been

No more next times
only now will do
lost opportunities
piled mountain high
until it is too late
regret filling the space
where dreams once lay
clouds of hope
turned to smog
leaving only a shadow
of what might have been.

A Loving Heart

Some days I feel
rebellious, disgruntled
don't want to do this anymore.
Then I take myself
some place quiet
to pray
my prayer of peace.

Dear Lord, calm my heart
open my eyes to all the blessings
I receive from You each day
fill my soul with serenity
knowing that You are
ever by my side
guiding, protecting, loving.

Restore my joy, my peace
so that I may ever
serve You with a loving heart.

The Game

Dog and cat
imagine that chase
is the game.
Dog always loses
cats are quick.

Power of Love

Oh, how your harsh words
burn and batter the soul
bitter, wrathful, full of resentment
they crush the hearts of others.

Ah, but kind words
sweet encouraging
free of judgement
lift the soul
with their quiet
comfort and love.

Holidays

Feasts, celebrations, holidays
yet one hour of heart
turned toward God
feels more joy than
earthly celebrations
can ever provide.

Power of Silent Prayer

Silent prayers are often
more honest than those
with many words.

Sit quietly in receptivity
open to hear the heart
of the Lord.

Empty Prayers

A prayer not followed
by action rings hollow and cold.
Allow prayer to open your heart
connect you to the Divine
that you then may go forth
and serve the Lord
with joy and gratitude.

All Hours

May I do Thy will
with an eager soul
dedicating my life
to Thy complete control

A loving prayer
to start my day
makes everything easier
along the way

Mid-day and evening
and all the hours between
may I worship you
my Lord, my King

Your Silent Heart

Pray with less and less
words until
only your silent heart
filled with love remains.

Heavenly Fragrance

The first act of my soul
as I awaken in a prayer
of gratitude which sweetens
my day, those few moments

with God fills me with peace
and strengthens me to
follow His direction
throughout the day.

The lingering moments
before sleep end my day
in contemplation
opening my heart to understand
what God would have me know.

I touch these moments with
tender prayers of gratitude
along the way infusing
my soul with the heavenly
fragrance of God's nearness.

Choose Well

C hoose the life you want
H ope leads to faith
O pen your heart to your inner voice
I ncorporate change with positive expectation
C ease to complain and judge
E xpect a miracle
S ee God's grace surrounding you

Bring Us Home
                      Bongo drums
                      keeps the beat

dancers circle
in full moon splendor
shaman guides
on healing journey
deep into the Great Beyond

All over the world
cultures have
healing rituals
as we seek for
body and soul

What longing
illness, need
pushes us to
the Divine
that calls within
a magnet
of love waits
for us to come
then bring us
home to serenity

Mouse in the House

A mouse in the house
creates a big alarm
while the elephant
in the dining room
brings cautious silence
everyone afraid

to admit it's there

Stars of Good Deeds

Unsung hero I am
never to know fame
until I'm dead
perhaps not even then

Good deeds need no glory
on earth for God puts
a star in the sky
each time we please Him
look to heaven
when you want to know
if God's pleased
for deeds well done

Broken Promises

Promises to keep
Don't make them if they're not true
Hearts break easily

Don't Settle for Less

Never settle for less
than your dreams

keep them ever as
your guiding star
for a heart without a dream
is a ship without a compass
a lover without
someone to love

D esign your life to fulfill your dreams
R ealize your dreams through commitment
E ach dream is a gift from God
A llow roadblocks to inspire you
M ake your dream come true with love

Golden Idols

How carefully we build
our golden idols
always searching
for peace within

If only we had
the love of our life
a bigger house
better job
more of this
or that
then we would
be content
maybe even happy

Beware you do not
become your idol

Put away your idols of want
seek only communication
with the Lord
for it is within His arms
we rest in serenity
only His love can
fill our hearts for
all else is fool's gold
glitter with no substance

Living Waters

Beware that God can
give us exactly what we want

Drink only from the cistern
of living waters
from the fount of the Holy Spirit

He who loves our Creator
will never thirst for God provides
for all our souls' need

No Darkness in the Light

The darkness cannot hide
from the Light
for even the smallest flicker
reveals that which

seeks to hide
in the darkness of its deeds.

Bathe me in Your Light, O God
that Darkness cannot come near.
Fill me with the light of Your love
that there be not even a thought
gone astray
that my heart be ever pure
that only Your love prevails
within me.

Lord's Day

The day of the Lord
is today, yea, every day
is the day we sing our
love and praise of our Creator
for out of gratitude
comes love

Let us walk in the Light
There is no God besides Me
saith the Lord
all I create is
one family
do not destroy
any man, animal
the very Earth
upon which you trod

Rather care for each other

no child shall go hungry
war, senseless slaying
is an abomination
for all I create is sacred
down to the tiniest flower

Heed these words
keep them in your heart
abide by them
for only love will prevail
only love will heal
this troubled world

Endless Chatter

Be still, quiet
the endless chatter
of a mind tha knows
no peace

Focus your thoughts
on the beauty of the Earth
scattered precision of the sky

Fill your mind
with loving thoughts
for we can choose
our thoughts, our feelings
when we focus on
all the beauty
and kindness in the world

Things I Can't Stand

        Roaches, rats, spiders
        snakes, people of color
        those of other religions
        fat people, skinny people
        people with birth defects
        homeless, drunkards
        drug addicts, prostitutes

        Is your hate list
        longer that your
        love list?

Impossible

I won't even try
M aybe you can but I can't
P ossibility is not in my vocabulary
O nce I tried it but I failed
S o I gave up
S ome people are luckier than I
I want to but I am afraid
B ut maybe I'll try again
L et's do it together
E ach success is a step for another success

No Time

Time—imagination segments
Time—squander or use wisely
What would life be like
if there were no
time delineations
a river to ocean of existence
spirit to infinity flow?

I don't have enough time
is an illusion
worse—an excuse.
We all make choices
that determine
the life we have.

Time—neither friend nor foe
endless flow
into the Great Beyond.

A Dot

A dot, a breath
small flicker
grain of sand
mote in a sunbeam
tiny speck of the Divine
therefore infinite
expanding into universes
that reach into infinity
and beyond.

Silent Desperation

I pretend I'm happy
paint a smiling face
laugh and joke around
nobody knows my pain
or sees the slices
I cover so they won't be found

I am a faceless teen
one of many you see
trying to understand
a world of insanity

bombs, drugs, expectation
people living in desperation
will there ever be
a safe world of love
for me

Lonely in Crowds

Being with people
makes me feel lonely
disconnected, afraid

While being in
a quiet place
free of the buzz

of frantic souls
I find my place
of serenity
where my soul
connects with
the Divine

These quiet times
with my Creator
cleanses me
fills me with faith
and gratitude
and brings me home

Where I Go

Everywhere I go
I see the hand of the Lord
even war-torn cities
have star splendor
blades of grass returning
random flowers
with sunshine faces
coming back, pushing
through man's destruction.

I feel God's presence
everywhere when I am ready
to let go of this world
to open my heart
my awareness

Dearest God
who is everywhere
comforting, guiding
to those of us
who surrender
our lives to You
help me to always
know you are ever
present even when
life seems too chaotic

Fill me with peace
with Your love and
Light that I may
ever serve You
as You would have
me do

Stop Doing It

The way to stop doing
something you know
is not good to do
is to stop doing it.

There are no magic cures
counseling reinforces
whining and self-pity
excuses

No, you simply must
STOP

stop looking for another way
and just do it
because you are tired
of carrying this burden

S ay no more—just do it!
T ake charge of who you want to be
O nly you can do what must be done
P ray for God to give you strength

God Speaks to Us

How does God speak to us?
I haven't seen a burning bush
no star has followed me
yet somehow I know I am
being guided wherever I go.

Sometimes God puts a desire
in my heart, a quiet language
other times there comes a knowing
of what I must do
opportunities come
that I hadn't anticipated
a gentle nudge, a feeling
of peace when I follow
these signs of God guiding me

Each of us must find
how to communicate
with the Divine
for your way may be

different from mine
but in every case we
must be willing
to open our hearts
to hear the silent
voice of our Creator

World of Music

Melodies of breezes
songs in the air
birds filled with song
music everywhere

Music heals, delights
expresses what we feel
leading us to the Beyond
to show us what is real.

Gone Astray

I'm living in a new world
but new only to me
where some may say a rock
I say a tree

That's a hat
for me, a cat
I think I'm losing
my mind

my world seems
lost in time

What happened
to old fashioned values
like integrity, modesty
honesty and faith

Has belief in God
become outdated
old fashioned, irrelevant
is this only a time
for revelry

Do not weep, God
though many
have gone astray
I still love You
for me, there's
no other way

Fade Away

Tell me I'm ready to hear
though I am blind and deaf
there is an inner world
of majesty
a world where I can
connect with the Divine
where peace and love
rules through all time

The distractions of the world
are fading one-by-one
in the light they melt away
gone are the markers
the cycles of night and day
there is only now
this moment in time
where I am in the matrix
of the sacred
merged with the Divine

Not My Job

Judging another is not my job
for who am I to find fault
when I, too, so often fail

Lord, fill my eyes with compassion
my heart with love
help me to understand
we are here to learn
often falling like toddlers
who need a helping hand

The life lesson is to learn
how to love
unconditionally, fully
as our Creator does
to move into His Light
merging, surrendering
becoming one with One
amen, amen, amen

Beware of the Trickster

Pick one, any one
magic tricks delight
Beware of the trickster
whose goal is to darken your light

How often we are fooled
by those whose work is to deceive
yet when we listen to our soul
the evil one we don't believe

Longing for Peace

Traffic sounds, planes overhead
TV blaring twenty-four hours a day
people shouting, lawn mowers
weed whackers, sirens going
garbage trucks, endless hours
of city noises

I long for the peace
of the floresta
for quiet walks on deserted beaches
moonlight walks dotted
only by an occasional
hoot of an owl nearby
stars generously sprinkled
across the sky

a time when there was
only God and me
yet I know He is
still with me
guiding me wherever I go
in the quiet of my heart
I am with Him, I know

Learning to Love

How do we learn to love
when our love is so tainted here?
Who can guide us
speak to our hearts
when the world seems
to only be focused
on greed and self-absorption?

No one of this world
no guru, master
no course, no CD, book
not even religion
for the only One who
has the Grace to lead
us on the path of love
resides within our hearts
gently calling, forgiving
and showing us what
endless love really is.

Nice

N ot going to be nice any more
I t's a lie that I'm always supposed to be nice
C an't love everyone, all the time
E nough is sometimes enough!

Rainbows

Rainbow--God's promise
Colors paint the sky with joy
Rainbows renew faith

Trapped?

I feel trapped
yet that is just
a feeling
feelings change
with intent

My intention
is to be peaceful
joyous, grateful
so I will keep
my focus on the Lord
for it is with Him
I find contentment
regardless of situation

I surrender, accept
what I cannot change
release all resentment
pray for strength
and faith
for others who need
the love and light

Internal Dialogue

How is it that our
internal dialogue
is so often filled with
complaints, gossip, judgement
worry, fear, discontentment
blah-blah-blah

This toxic chatter dulls
our awareness of the joys
that surround us
simple pleasure we
have every day
often unobserved
because we have
forgotten how to laugh
be grateful
loving
how to open our hearts
to the light which
calms the soul

Oh, Lord, may I always

be grateful, loving
Joyous filled with
Your love forever more

It's Your Fault

Let's play the blame game
it's your fault!
not my fault
self-righteousness
leads the way

No situation can be changed
by indignation and blame
whatever happened—let it go
figure out what needs to
be done to correct the situation
and do it with a loving heart

B less the situation with God's love
L isten to the other with compassion
A lways ask God to guide in resolving conflict
M ake a promise to yourself to stop blaming
E very situation has a loving resolution

God at Play

Puffy cloud float by
Its shape changes with the breeze
God likes to play, too

God Knows

Rain or sun today
Either one is fine with me
God knows what we need

Embroidery Lesson

Mama always said
Take it out, do it again
Good enough won't do

Housework Therapy

Cleaning therapy
Mopping floors heals resentment
House and heart sparkles

Mama's Answer

When she disapproved
Silence was her response
Message loud and clear

Autumn

I'm letting go
red leaves of pain
yellow leaves of sorrow
faded green of lost faith
down, down, down they fall
to transform into
renewed soil
to bring forth
new life full
of expectation of joy

Life cycles again
until we learn to trust
that all is part of
God's plan

Love versus Judgement

Hatred comes from judgement
for when we accept a person
as he is at that moment
it becomes unconditional love
which expands to eternity

Judgement subtracts, lessons
not those we judge but ourselves
love expands those we love
as well as our own souls

Claiming Our Idols

What is our idol
anything we desire
that is beyond our necessity
power, wealth recognition
food, booze, ambition, possessions
more poisons us, feeding
our desires into addictions

Only love can be claimed
in ever increasing amounts
Divine love…unconditional
endless

Envy to Inspiration

How does envy become
inspiration?
By eliminating envy
the success of others
can serve as inspiration
for us to continue toward
our worthy goals
being happy for the other person

How We Perceive

I am afraid
what if…..

I am uncertain
what an adventure

How often our perception
of situations is what
colors how we react to them

Fear and Doubt

Fear and doubt paralyzes us
yet God's plan and power
moves us along,,, builds
our trust and courage
weakness pushing us
to rely, to draw near
our loving Creator of All

Even if you feel afraid
just do it
for God's grace will
help you every step of the way
all things are possible
when we walk in the Light
of our Lord

Boys versus Girls

Pretty
sweet, charming, obedient
little girls

tough
brave, mischievous, strong
boys will be boys
gender gap

Love Me as I Am

Today I'm a lion
tomorrow a mouse
courageous yet shy
I am but
I can only be
who I am right now
perhaps I will change
but I don't know how

Please love however I am
for, really, I'm doing
the best I can

Tomatoes

Tomatoes
red, juicy, full of summer sun
fresh from the garden
never a can
if we eat what's grown locally
by season
we remember what food
tasted like when we were young

Candles

Candles
romantic, sacred, beautiful
flattering, mood setting
energy efficient

Turn out the lights
light candles instead
se the world
in a different way
sometimes we just need
a different perspective

More Stuff?

Do you want this
yes or no
simple decisions
are often the most difficult
but when it comes
to more stuff
say "no"

Can't See Him

I don't believe in God

because I can't see Him
but I believe in air
electricity, political promises
and the lottery

Divine Matrix
Creator of All
One of many names
all of which is One

Sending Out

Sending out
letting it ring
singing voice and heart
Light and Love
illuminating
this world of darkness
candle by candle

Today

Just for today
for there is only now
be at peace
this moment is ripe
with wonder for
How great is our God
let His glory fill you
grant you serenity

fill you with love
everlasting

Halloween

Halloween
of the devil
trick or treat
what message are we
giving our children
celebration all in good fun
or is it?

Symbols

How important are symbols?
Do they trigger certain responses
can they be used for
good or bad?

S acred or wicked
Y in and Yang
M ore powerful than we realize
B eware of their impact
O pen only to those with positive energy
L ight and love are clearly perceived

Don't Know

It's okay to say "I don't know."
Because Cortana can look it up
we've gotten too lazy
to even Google.
Where's my robot?
Drones kill, too
and are not buried in Arlington.

What is "real" in this world
mechanical people
on layers of phone menus?
Are all the people in Walmart
for real—sometimes
it's hard to tell

Can't Sleep

If I can't sleep
am I sick, need a pill
or just a good book
and a willingness
to listen to my body?

Facebook, watching "news"
endless shopping
for things we don't need

What are we putting
into life?

When we die, will anyone
notice?

What Is Praise?

Glory to God!
Why do we praise God?
Does His ego need
validation?
Of course not!

Praise stems from joy
from gratitude
humbled awe of God's grace.
Let the world praise God
with joined hearts and hands
that never again shall
we die of hatred and greed.

Praise the One, the only God
Creator of All
Each grain of sand
star above
sunsets and sunrises
across the globe
tiny babies in wombs

May our hearts be so filled
that they overflow
with joy and gratitude
our voices raised
in songs of sweet surrender.

Doing the Best I Can

I am here, Lord
perhaps a little shaky
in faith at times
sometimes a bit fearful
but I am here, Lord

Not as patient
as I want to be
still judgmental
but I am here, Lord
loving You
worshiping You
Doing the best I can

Do Dreams Come True?

Do thoughts become
reality
must they be shaped
like prayer
do thoughts and prayers
draw to us
that which we desire?

Our list of pleas
grows long.

Who is listening
fairy Godmother
genies in bottles
lucky four leaf clovers

Seven billion people
praying, beseeching
what a clatter
who listens
who cares
yet we continue
hoping, knowing
sensing God's presence
within and without
when we stop
sit in quiet expectation
to listen to the voice
of our Creator, God of All

My God Is Love

My God is love
love cannot be vengeful
play favorites
demand living sacrifices

True love is pure
full of grace
non-judgemental
filled with compassion
merciful
love is God

and I who comes
from God
needs to learn
how to love
not a semblance of love
rather as God loves
pure and unconditional

I'm so far away from
being this kind of love
but I'm trying
and with God's grace
will know and be
this kind of love
someday

Little Lessons

A child's laughter
a puppy's play
innocent, redeeming
reminding us
if only we care
to learn

Soup

Soup
comforting, warm on a cold night
made with love, shared

winter delight

Pickles

Pickles
sweet or sour
sliced in sandwiches
or eaten alone
companion to all
crunchy delight

Playful Melodies

Sing for your supper
Playful melodies delight
Music is magic

Who Is Right?

Each religion
is sure they are "right"
whole cultures believe
their customs show
the correct way to live
political beliefs are
sacred cows
all "truths" are
the only way to believe

So, who is right?
maybe all
maybe none

Do we destroy all
who do not think
as we do?
Does our God condemn
all to eternal damnation
those who do not embrace
our beliefs?

I have but one belief:
God is Love
only Love
eternally
everything else
is speculation

I also want to be Love
not feel love
be Love
unequivocally
eternally

Happy or Sad

Today I'm happy
or perhaps sad
either way
I am glad

that I have this day
sunshine, flowers
stars at night
will still be here
regardless of how I feel
for this I am grateful
happy or sad

Nothing Is Mine

Nothing is mine
things come and go
what I have today
perhaps someone needs more

Material goods don't have to stay
for love from the heart
lasts through eternity
making me rich
day by day

On Tip Toes

Walking on tip toes
reaching high
quietly I pass
into the sky

Sometimes I'm here
then I disappear

you may think I'm gone
but then I'm near

who am I
what am I
that I come and go
a cloud that moves
with the wind
wherever it may blow

Winding Down

Winding down
going slower
choosing better
how I want to
spend my time

Leaving time
to just be
time with no
have to…

Had to learn
how to just be
without needing to do
why is this so hard?

Magic happens
when there is grace
for it to blossom
grace discovered

treasured
received

One Word Poem

One
word
poem
LOVE

nothing
else
needed

Play

Play
cats and puppies
know how
I'm studying both
wondering why
I forgot

Through the Valley of Death

"Yea, though I walk through
the valley of death"
most people have experienced

hard times
hopelessness
paralyzing fear
yet we've had the strength
to go on

There is a Source
a Fount from which
we can draw
fortitude, serenity, faith

The portal lies within
loving intention
opens the door
within we find the Light
heartbeat of love
that conquers all
and reminds us
that God is by our side
to guide us through
whatever we face
with grace and love
through all eternity
and into the Great Beyond

Sleep

Sleep
restful, refilling, refreshing
sleep
restless, dreams of fear
hours where sleep

cannot be found
Today I am grateful
for sleep that restores
pain-free, serene, rejuvenating

S nores fill the house
L ots of street noises
E ven the house makes squeaks and groans
E ach minute drags by
P ieces of worry floating by

S erene hours
L et's my body restore
E ven birds and animals sleep
E ach night of restful sleep is precious
P eaceful sleep is a blessing

Again

Seems like I forgot
So I will try to recall
Memory blips again

Except When I Don't

I have great faith
except when I don't
I am a pillar of strength
who sometimes
trembles with fear

Wisdom fills my words
then I speak like a fool
I have moments of
profound goodness
yet they soon fade away

A kaleidoscope is my soul
and yet there is this
steady pulse within
a knowing so profound
that nothing changes
this place filled with
the Light of Divinity

When I dwell in the light
all confusion disappears
pain, fear, anger, envy
disappears for Light
banishes all darkness
love, the alchemy
of resolution
there is only love
all else is illusion

Hope or Faith

Hope or faith
intention versus expectation
words, more words
never enough words
to try to explain
that which IS

When the knowing
comes
I know
unshakably
unmistakably

I know
God is Love
only love
eternal love
consistent, unconditional

Regardless of what
I do or don't do
think, believe, hope
God is Love
God
is
LOVE

Why I Forgive

I forgive because
I should not judge
I forgive
not to be liked
I forgive
for doing so
sets me free
of resentment
granting me serenity

I forgive—not for the other
but rather for me

Lost Tears

I cannot find my tears
where have they gone
my broken heart
is missing, too
Now I laugh
for I've forgotten
what I thought
was so important then

Love Me?

Will you love me
if I don't agree with you?
Can we have different
ideas, views, opinions
or is our love so fragile
that it cannot withstand
differences in the color
of skin, belief, about
issues of the soul
cultural and political
differences?

Is love ever fragile
judgmental, accusing

hateful, killing
conditional in any way?

a resounding NO!

Love is love
nothing else

and until we become
Love
(note the noun, not verb)
then what we call love
is not love

Be Love

Love on a Stick

Sunshine on a stick
Lollipop that tastes like love
Eat one a day

Open the Window

Open the window
let in fresh air
listen to the birds
feel the warmth of the sun

Sometimes it is as easy

as opening a window
to let God into your life

Put aside your what-ifs
act as if you believe
until your doubts fade away

God is

God is love

Invite Him into your life
let His love fill you
until all hurt disappears
and you become love, too

Who You Are

Do not define yourself
by your failures
to do or not do
for your are not
impatient, sinful
envious, naught, bad

These labels are even
their actions
are not who you are
regardless of earthly
circumstances

For you are a soul

a Divine fragment
of glory
designed and created
by our Creator
whom we call by
many names
God Jehovah
Allah, Spirit
I AM that I AM
and you are holy
a soul—be who you are

Integrity?

Would I if I could
and get away with it?
Probably
so much for integrity

Love Signals

Eyes passing love
No words spoken
Love signals

Broken Promises

Unkempt promises

Integrity broken
Almost impossible to mend

True Failure

True failure
is when
you never even
tried

Maybe—the Lie

Maybe usually means
no, but I don't
want to tell you

Which One?

If someone is smart
but acts stupid
is he smart or stupid?

People Pleasing

Pleasing people
without lying

is almost impossible

Don't trade integrity
for fleeting approval

Lower Your Eyes

Lower your eyes, men
clean-up your thoughts
a woman with appeal
is not an invitation

You are responsible
for the impurity
of your thoughts

What's the Difference?

"I give up" speaks of defeat
we need not let
circumstances we can't
change tear us down
for God has promised
us to comfort and guide
protect and love
us without fail

I surrender
trusting I will have
the strength and faith

to accept with serenity
that which I must
walk through
knowing all I experience
presents me with
chances to learn
grow and experience
the richness of life

I surrender
joyously or not
to God's will
and with my
willingness
to surrender
I find peace

Stubborn

S urely my way is best
T ry to make me change--can't
U seless is your opinion
B lind am I to other possibilities
B utting heads where 'er I go
O ne day I may change
R ealize I might be wrong
N eed to learn to trust the Lord

Impossible

What seems impossible to me
is easy for the Lord
God's omnipotence
is not hypothetical

He does not need
our belief
rather He offers
His unending love
which we must accept
or not

Nothing is impossible
by the Hand of
He who is One
for there is none
besides Him

Harden Heart

Beware for your hardened heart
may result in you receiving
your heart's desire

Make not excuses
but rather obey
the guidance of the Lord

I'm too weak, too afraid

can't do this, don't want
to do that

Though you may be
all of these
your God is not
trust in Him
to bring you through
the challenges you face
for He is Creator of all
a loving Source
all that is good
God is love
God is God
God is

What's the Difference?

Cry baby
baby cry
not the same at all
chin up!

One More

Sweet potatoes
baked in a pie
a touch of lemon
begs for another piece

How Gossip Starts

A secret
is more fun
when shared
soon making it
gossip

Justice

Justice
is too close to revenge
compassion
is closer to love

The Penalty

The penalty lasts forever
think carefully first
soul scar

Who Me?

Who me?
yes, you

being afraid
doesn't get you
an excuse
for God will always
help you if you ask

Strength comes with prayer

When Do We Finish?

People, person, you
me, I
who is responsible
who cares
who does not?

Let someone else do it
I've already done my share
when have we done enough?

When it is done
we've done enough
our contribution
does not depend
on what anyone else
does or does not do.

Exactly

Exactly—get it right

more or less
is not good enough
only your best will do

Buy More

Buy more
closets overflowing
buy more
can't fill up the hole
can't buy what you need
to stop feeling
like you need more
only God's love
will satisfy
don't need to buy it
just ask to receive

Tapping

Tap, tap, tap
jiggle some more
always in motion
never sit still
energy wasted
going no where

Evil—Part of the Plan?

Is evil part of God's plan
cruelty, abuse, dark deeds?
"I'm going to create a world
let people decide
if there is to be good and bad."
Why make us capable of evil?
Is life a virtual reality game
for a bored creator?

Will I be damned
for thinking such a thought?

Each of us have moments
when we shout, "Why God?"
It's then that I pray
God, grant me peace
help me let go of what
I don't understand.

God is Love
I always come
back to this.

I sit in my sandbox
play with my toys
knowing only
God is love
the rest I don't
understand
or need to.

Forget It

Forget it
I's over
don't need to relay it
again and again
block it out
with prayer
which brings serenity
when we give to God
that which troubles
our soul.

Never Say Never

I wouldn't if I could
there are some things
I'd never do

While this may be true
I've eaten "never"
several times
and now know
we do not know
how we would react
until the opportunity comes
and the cock has crowed
three times

Smiling Faces

Evil wears a smile
Beware of smiling faces
Use discernment, please

Empathy

E veryone has opportunities to feel empathy
M any times we've hardened our hearts
P eople can so demanding
A lways look at your motivation
T ruth is not always so clear
H elping requires discernment
Y our choice depends on you

Communicating with the Soul

One's eyes must
cease to see
ears no longer hear
lips speak only silence

Until only the sweet
communicating
with our Creator
satisfies our soul

A Moment in Time

Today, a tiny moment
in a fragile life
not even a star flicker
in the concept of time
yet today is magnificent
I am alive in a world
of great beauty

Filled with opportunity
a moment in time
so special if I use
it well, it can cause
a ripple that moves
into eternity

Your Full Attention

Give me your full attention
don't "multi-task" when
I am speaking from my heart.

One of the greatest gifts
we can give each other
is our full attention.

Most people long for connection
an honest, loving, non-judgmental
conversation, a sharing of souls.

How rare this is but

how very precious
turn off the TV, Internet
sit and talk about
what's in your heart
listen carefully, fully
when the other person speaks
and you will discover
what loving communication
really is about.

Behind the Wall

Can I share
an unacceptable view
one that is contrary
to yours or must I only speak when
we are in agreement?

Can I sit comfortably
on the sidewalk
with one who lives on the street?
Can we talk
openly about why
I live in a comfortable
house while he is dirty
hungry, friendless, homeless?

Is my judgment
complacency
self-centeredness
a wall behind
which I hide

too afraid to love
and be vulnerable?

What's Coming?

summer is all gone
autumn leaves patchwork the ground
then comes dreaded snow

Chains of Fear

Anger–fear
self-righteousness–fear
complacency–fear

We are fear-filled beings
seeking anything
that with relieve
even momentarily
the fear that binds

Yet there is only
one thing that
can free us
give us a life
of serenity
Love
of our Creator
each other
sets us free

of the chains
of fear

I Am Light

I am Light
yes, so are you
all part of the Eternal Light

Do not think you
could not possibly be
so tired, full of errors for
you are Light
I am, too

Nothing can change this
for we are Light
and Light is forever
nothing dims Light
it is just is
so are you
so am I
so are we
LIGHT

Indiscriminate Love?

What is indiscriminate love?
Discernment is one of the
spiritual gifts but how

does one know who not
to love? Who are the unlovables?

There are certainly
people we should avoid
dangerous people with
evil intent
yet even they deserve
our prayers, even our help
if we can do it safely.

Perhaps the idea of
indiscriminate love
is confusing because
it isn't really love.

Love is pure
without ulterior motive
never self-serving
true love is from the Divine
Love is God
God is Love.

What Steals Your Joy?

Discontent, resentment
ingratitude will steal
your joy.

"I have learned
in whatever situation
I am to be content"

How does one feel
contentment
in difficult situations?

There is an inner core of us
where lies true serenity.
When there, we understand
that all of this life is temporary
providing opportunities
to learn patience, compassion
how to be in such a state
of Divine love
that we never move
out of that place
regardless of what is
happening in the outer world.

Most Fragile Times

When do I stop questioning
let go of doubts
confusion
skepticism?

I will let them go
trust that inner voice
to guide me in all I do.

No more theories
doctrines, should
can't , sins, guilt, fear

Only the peace of the Divine
guiding me, protecting
love me
even at my most fragile times.

How Big

How big is big
oceans, universes, eternity
how long is eternity
what is beyond it
the immensity of God
is beyond comprehension
yet He knows me, loves me

I…so insignificant
but not to God

The Cactus

Mean, grouchy, disagreeable
a cactus
but even a cactus
has beautiful flowers
under the right conditions

Don't give up on anyone

Who I Really Am

I clap, give a pretend smile
play the game
say I do when I don't
wonder why I am
discontented, frustrated
I want to be authentic
not a shadow of someone else
but do I know
who I am, really am?

Beyond the Veil

Walking beyond the veil
in the world of beyond
seeing what cannot be seen
knowing the unknown
understanding the illusion
we call "life"

Returning to this world
changed in ways that
cannot be discussed
need not be talked about
for each need to experience
this in their own way.

Becoming My Dog

      I am becoming my dog
      a loving, contented guy
    simple needs, not concerned
     about the past or future
    playful, joyful, values naps

       I have a ways to go
       but I love to eat
     as much as he does
      so at least I've
      mastered that.

Noise

N oise—anything that disturbs
O nce you've learned to love silence
I nstances of soothing noise
S ilence opens the heart to hear God
E njoy the serenity of silence

From the Lord

      Be kind
    it's so easy
  to be unkind
   thoughtless

Be compassionate

for truly
there but for the
grace of God
go you or I

Be of good cheer
spread the joy
of the Lord
to those in Darkness

Be loving to all
creatures that God
has made
for life is sacred
all come from the Lord

In and Out

Swimming, gliding
moving in and out
of this world
perhaps another
into what others call
reality which seems
like illusion

I am so much more
than what you think
I am even more
than what I think
I AM

I am not Walmart
nor Burka
no shaman on
a full moon

Not redwoods
nor ancient healing cedars
a rare cactus bloom
I am not here
nor there
yet am through
all eternity
for I am Source
and you are, too
waiting, unfolding
becoming
who we already are

You Poked My Heart

You poked my heart
my heart
now it bleeds tears
all the sorrow
I have held inside
hoping no one
would ever notice

From the Lord

Be kind
it's so easy
to be unkind
thoughtless

Be compassionate
for truly
there but for the
grace of God
go you or I

Be of good cheer
spread the joy
of the Lord
to those in Darkness

Be loving to all
creatures that God
has made
for life is sacred
all come from the Lord

Not Ready

Too many, too much
not ready
although you say I am

My world has circles
of reality, layers, if you will

none is right
nor is wrong
all is our perception
mixed with intention
creating our reality

Perhaps there is no
you or me
only they
or nothing at all
except for One

Lord, Close My Mouth

Lord, close my mouth
when I need to be silent
open it when I need to speak
sometimes it is hard to know
the difference
unless You guide me…
when I let You

Going, Going, Gone

Crawling in a worm hole
in the sky
going, going, gone

Where are You?

Every where

Then where am I
that I cannot see You?

I have made you blind
so you can see Me
with your heart.

One at a Time

Corn on a cob
rows all in a line
how do you eat them
one row at a time?

I am methodical
nothing else will do
one step at a time
I am looking for you

Beginning or end
not to be found
let go of the convention
for you are not bound

Let your spirt go
so it can finally know
the sacred, the profound
waiting to be found.

My Shoes

Well-traveled, comfortable, protecting
some don't have what we take for granted
today I'll be grateful
for my unappreciated shoes

Blue

Blue
sky, mood, bird
choose which you want to be
always choose joy

B e happy
L ove creates peace
U nlock your heart
E ach day is filled with blessings

Doggie Bag

Wrap it up
take it home
left-overs
become a dog feast

No Peace on Earth

Peace on Earth
is not meant to be
we're here to learn
how to move
to reality

Paint a Picture

Paint a picture
create a symphony
become all that we
are meant to be

Perhaps nothing grand
is who I AM
a simple soul
with no special goal

He Is Light

In Him, there is
no darkness at all
God is Light—pure Light
no shadow can be
where there is Light

God is Light
He is Love

when we walk with Him
we are Light
away from the Dark we flee

I—the Enemy

I am the enemy
for no one has ever done
as bad to me as I do
to myself

I won't lie to you
declaring how honest I am
but constantly lie to myself
promises easily made
are soon broken

I tiptoe around
the pious image I project
when my heart is filled
with resentment
judgement and smoldering
ashes of past hurts

Cleanse me, O Lord
free me from all
that keeps Your Light

The Prisoner

In a box
safe from all
my secure haven
becomes my prison
walls that keep others out
keep me in
afraid to love
to trust
a prisoner
longing to be set free

The Bubble

I am a bubble
filled with
surrounded by
over-flowing
with light

Floating across
darkened universes
bringing Light
where 'er I go

Sad Poem

Sad poem
can hold

keys to joy
for they make
one stop
to count one's blessings
changing the sad story
with gratitude

Life goes on

Our Memorial

Farmers, keepers
of the earth
holders of ancient
knowledge of wisdom

So many have been removed
from the knowing of nature
losing respect and understanding
of the fine balance of ecosystems

Ignorance cannot
be excused
for trees still die
rivers and oceans
become cesspools
even the air hangs
heavy in the sky

Mankind—destroyer of all
change your greedy ways
or soon you also perish

in the pollution you have
created, a broken
memorial to selfishness

A Little Honest

How honest do you
want to be today
tell the truth
nothing but the truth
or a few whoppers
sandwiched in, garnished
by a few white lies?

Integrity cannot
be subdivided.
An untruth is a lie
no matter how you
call it
honesty—all or nothing
you can't be a little pregnant
nor can you be partly honest.

Winter's Gift

Warm sweaters, hot tea
a fireplace chat with a friend
winter's cozy gift

Holograms of God

Hologram of God
Soul featuring the Divine
Our body's a shell

Sleeping Dogs

Dog
running in his sleep
giving little yelps
of pleasure or pain
should I wake him
hard to decide
sleep doggie sleep

Another Time

Some days I don't feel kind
other days I feel just fine
think I'll stay in bed
pull the covers over my head
I'll be kind another time

Cold Feet

Cold feet, no sweetheart
gonna' find some warm socks

and try again

Knowledge Without God

"Knowledge without God
can only produce
smarter sinners"

Always learning
never knowing
where is truth
to be found

Are we the terminal
generation end of times
destined to destruction
by our own hand?

How do we stop
this run-away train?
There is a Power
who can change
this story
so simple
yet few will do

The gift of Love
can heal it all
but it's up to
me and you.

Each must do

his part—surrender
to love in all you do

There is a better way.

One Little Candle

One little candle
pushes the darkness away
each flame of love counts

Simple Math

One and one are two
in yester-year
worked then, why not now?

Source of Light

How can one live
without our God
how hopeless
this world would be

I walk in the Light
in this world of darkness
shadows sometimes
tugging me

I walk in the Light
even when I fail
He guides me
to try again

God is Light
I am, too
a soul created
from the Source
of all pure love

You also
come from Source
awaken and unfold
with love
for eternity

No Explanation Needed

God cannot be explained
analyzed, foot-noted
rationalized, dismissed
God is
with or without your belief

God does not need
our prayers and praise
we need them
He said "I AM"
not " I am if… or when…"

God is
It is we-you and I
who must come to Him
humbly, in surrender
with gratitude
full of honest intuition
hearts open
ready to be filled
with Light and Love

God is
Light
Love

Going to Market

Going to the market
To see what I can buy there
From the Love Garden

Finally

Finally I see her pain
not her anger
rather her helplessness
her fear
of being alone, rejected
not good enough
not in the eyes of others
but in her own eyes

in her core
because she has not yet
seen the beauty of her soul

Finally I see in her
myself

Walking That Line

Woman-child
walking that line
is not easy
oh how you suffer
in those highs and lows
17 and 70
we are at opposite
ends of life
I prefer my time
for it is now
that I understand
serenity and gratitude
a time of loving
with the soul

Bleeding

Bleeding
life slipping away
even the tears are red
emptying out of this broken vessel

freeing the soul
to return home

Push and Pull

Push
shove
push
pull
tug-of-war
see-saw
up and down
balance is
hard to find
and maintain

Going Home

Is it time to go?
I'm ready
bags packed
waiting
finished here

Don't give me more, Lord
still need me here, You say
unpacking my bag, Lord
wishing I could
come home to You

> You are home, my child
> for I am always with you
> wherever you go
> is home when your
> heart is with Me.

Soon

> I will
> soon
> I'll try
> soon
> gonna' get around to it
> soon
> be right there, Lord
> soon

I Promise

> I'm full of promises
> so easy to make
> not hard at all
> I've going to change this
> I promise
>
> Keeping them is the trick
> there've been a few
> but not very many
> I'm going to change this

I promise

Chatterbox Head

Chatterbox head
always complaining
criticizing all
robbing my peace

I smile and nod your way
but that annoying voice
finds fault so easily
hiding the quiet voice
that speaks only of love

Two voices
whichever I choose
the other will fade away

Religion for Sale

When did worship
become entertainment
profitable
full of rhetoric
with not much love?

Religion for sale
only one is right
all the rest to eternal damnation

does God really have a preference
no—He just wants us to love

Babies and Dogs

What do babies
and dogs think about
that they are so
serene and joyous

Yet we walk around
with negative chatter
in our minds, complaints
resentment, fear

How does one put
the outside smile
inside to quiet
our demons

We don't
for serenity
comes from the heart
joy is found there, too
for there is the Source
of who we really are

When I am still
go within
to the place
of contentment
I find the Light

which is always there.

I am at peace

Our Integrity

The treasure of integrity
when broken
is hard to mend

Make your work sacred
I say, I do
for honor should be
guarded well

Do not break your word
especially to yourself

"In God do we trust"
but can we trust ourselves

Cat-in-the-Lap

Cat in a lap
Purring with contentment
Sometimes life is so simple

Violent Games

Games that kill people
are not games
thou shalt not kill
is all inclusive

Witches Riding

Witch on a broomstick
riding across the full moon
the dark soul's delight

Pretending

We pretend we are
One way then act another
We lie to ourselves

Labels

A label for all
Making us less a person
I am who I AM

No Explanation Needed

When I say "No"
Do not ask again
Nor do I have to explain

Respect All

Respect each other
Under all circumstances
Good rule to live by

Why Do Good

Do people do good
out of fear
to feel good about themselves
for the approval of others
including God?

Goodness cannot be
bought—not even with
good deeds for true goodness
needs love to make it grow

Ironically, being kind
helping others—even
without a loving heart
can sometime spark
that light within

bringing forth ab innate
Light waiting to be released
from a soul ready to unfold

G reat is the power of love
O nly you can change yourself
O pen your heart to find your goodness
D o good unto others and yourself as well

Do You Care?

Do you know
or even care?
Can you see
hear, feel
or is your world
only you?

Mine, me
seldom you
never we
this should
never be

We are not
separate
rather past
of a whole

If we do not
help take care of all
we subtract from

ourselves as well

Trees falling
men, too
babies hungry
what shall we do?

No Home

This house
is not a home
for in it dwells
no love

We go through
the motions of living
yet do not have a life

This house
is not a home
until we learn
how to love
each other

Will I ever
have a home?
Do you?

New Beginnings

New beginnings
I try once again
am I making
any progress
or repeating
what I didn't learn?

Dancing in the Moonlight

Let's dance in the moonlight
sing songs to the stars
play with the fairies
be who we really are

Full of joy
such fools who do not see
the bad
every day's a happy day
when we refuse to see
the sad

Things I know

Things I know are true
sun comes up every day
trees bear fruit
that are theirs to bear
rivers flow to the sea

God loves you and me

We live, we die
that's for sure
the truth we seek
is love that's pure

God is pure love
it's the truth
to which I cling
to love like Him
what joy it would bring

Time to Go

Voices and faces
are growing dim
while my desire for You
increases, brightens

I am forgetting
yet remembering
Your love for me
thank-you for
forgetfulness

I am walking slower
and seeing more
feeling the breeze
on my skin
the bird singing
its mating song

Thank-you, Lord
for this time
to reflect
before it is
my time to go

No Name

I lay my name aside
you need to use it no more
how can you name
the light from the sun
stars, a candle
for Light needs no name
unless you want to
call it Love

Too Many Books

Thousands of books
I have read
did not teach me
the one thing I
long to know
how to love You
so much that
I am only complete
when I fully comprehend
Your love

and that
We are One

What I Am and Am Not

All the things
I think I am
I'm not
then who am I
what am I
the eternal question

So many religions
myths, philosophies
but do they know

How does one believe
when one does not
are we so good
at self-deception

I have sifted out
a nugget of truth
by which I live
and return to this
knowing again and again
God is Love
pure love
Light
incapable of wrong

All else falls away

in this singular truth

Less and Less

A simple life
less and less
instead of more
time moving slowly
letting go of
doing
now—being

Savoring the sun
on my face
gardenias in the air
an orange eaten
in tiny bites

Bits of life
instead of gulps
taking time
to be grateful
for all

S ee with your heart
I gnore that which distracts
M ake each moment a special memory
P ay attention to your blessings
L et social demands fall away
E ach day is a lifetime

Reaffirm Our Goodness

Let's focus
on our goodness
reaffirm our souls
instead of clinging
to the idea of sin

There is much good
in the world
let that light
shine, banishing
all darkness which
flees from the Light

Our Creator made us
with souls of love
sparks of light
which illuminate
like winter stars
across the sky

No Definition

Love cannot be explained
sometimes we try by saying
what it's not
trying to say what it is
always limits love

Love is a way of being
not doing

be love
pure love
without limit
explanation
or conditions
be love
be

Just One Little Candle

In a world where
places of worship
and schools are
targets for terror
where greed
replaces compassion
there are still
fields of flowers
glorious blankets of stars
people who care

Even one little moment of light
can dispel darkness
a second cancels more

Let us join our lights
across the globe
to cancel the dark
which must always vanish
in the presence
of Light—Source
of Love

Creator of All

Sins of Old

My morning coffee
So few sins are left for old
Quick! Pour the coffee

Pickle Poem

P ut on a sandwich
I nvite their sweet or sour taste
C runch, flavorful
K iss a pickle
L et's share our pickles
E ach country has their own kind
S mile a pickle smile

Sweet or sour
Pickles save the day
though often
are targets of jest

Picture a pickle
the perfect gift
for someone
with no sense
of humor

Garden of Sorrow

There is a Garden of Sorrow
where broken promises
are laid to rest
a place where children
lose their innocence
adults their hope

Come to the tree
of endless hopeless
where ghosts play
in the shadow

Oh, Garden of Sorrow
unspoken words
unshed tears
shadows of yesterdays

Never Forgive

Sometimes we never forget
never ever do we forgive
living forever in our self-made
sorrow and regret

Disrespect

When you disrespect someone
you do not decrease their value

only your own

Finally Free

Floating
slipping by
letting go
of all that
bogs me down
finally
I am free

The Hat

Hat
cover:
hair loss
too much sun
bad hair day

And you thought
it was a fashion
statement

Who Can I Trust?

Meat thermometer
tells when it's done

as long as you always
want it cooked
the same way

Day of Rest

Day of rest
each week
seems like
only God
knows how
important
this is

Stoned

Stoned
escape from life's stresses
keeps one stuck spiritually
no growth is possible
stresses are lessons
in disguise

1000 Cuts

Death by a thousand cuts
Delivered by a tongue
Slays the body and soul

P-Nut Butter

Peanut butter
Keeps them licking
My dog's favorite treat

Twist of Fate

Do not pass me by
without acknowledging
my existence
a simple nod
let your eyes
meet mine
if you feel
compassion
at best
or spiritual
connection
give me a smile
for I am you
with a quick
twist of fate
and you are me
in desperate need
for someone to care
that I exist

Lord, Give Me a Hand

The load's too heavy
mountain too steep
I am old and bent
back and knees
not so good
can't hear too well
almost blind
the load's
too heavy
Lord, please give
me a hand

Praise the Lord
I'm finally free
of a load too big
for an aching knee
a soul come home
who rests in Thee

Humble Heart

I'm learning to have
a humble heart
such a hard lesson for me
there's a very fine line
between humility and
arrogance
self-respect and
self-centeredness
each choice shows

where I am

Dear Lord
please guide me
may I have the strength
and wisdom to choose well
that I may have a humble heart
worthy to give You
just as I am

Follow the Crowd

Standing true
to who I am
I have no need
to follow you

How can we "belong"
part of the group
yet still keep
our integrity?

Lord, stay close by
keep me strong
great is my need to belong
help me to know
You're always near
that I am never alone

To Motherhood

To all mothers
whose hearts are
full of sorrow
wondering if we failed
when our children
go wrong

Who is the blame
if a child
goes astray
the mother's always to blame

Yet each of us make choices
all our lives that lead
us where we are
not the mother or father
not society
video games
but a soul who chooses
to ignore the Light
preferring the deeds of Dark
while a mother weeps
and wonder what she did wrong

The answer, of course
is nothing
she did the best she could

Respect

Courtesy preferred
Though you don't have to like me
Respect is a must

Those in Need

Helping those in need
Helps us to learn compassion
Gives us gratitude

A Moment in Time

Open your heart
let love in
do not be afraid

Open your door
go into the world
do not be afraid

Ask what you can do
to change the world
even if only a moment
in time for goodness
ripples like waves
traveling around the world
do not be afraid
to let the light of love

shine through you even
if only for a moment in time

Life's Gifts

May apples hide under their leaves
little gifts often unfound
for we must look carefully
to see them

Too often we miss
the many gifts
life brings us
for unless we live carefully
we pass them by

Your Grace, Your Miracle

Today I will not complain
or criticize—no, really, I mean it!

I will remain in loving silence
when provoked
God, I need help with this one

I will channel all negative
thoughts to the Light
exchange them for loving prayer
Lord, only with Your grace
can I do this

Most of all, God
I want to always act
from a position of love
the pure love You demonstrate
this requires Your miracle
in my life
which You offer
when I am
willing to receive

Just Try

I am not ready
this lesson is too hard
give it to someone else
further down the path

We all have felt
ill-prepared for what
we are experiencing
yet we can grow into
each task we receive

One step at a time
we learn to walk
we fall, get up, fall again
keep trying until
one day it becomes natural

If we wait until

we are ready to try
we never get there

No Saint Nor Sage

No saint am I
nor am I a sage
foolish me, full of pride
rebellious
unwilling to conform
yet I am also
loving and kind
willing to learn
even when I resist

Lord, have patience
with your wayward child
I'm doing the best I can
with still a long way to grow

In Music

I snuggle in music
when I am sad
sing it from the housetops
when I am glad
music is the language
of my soul
a gift of life
I never take for granted

M akes me joyous
U nlocks my heart
S inging releases serenity
I nsitlls a sense of peace
C ures just about everything

Seek to Grow

I will pour out my Spirit
upon you
listen well for I am
with you
trust that
I will guide you
beyond the beyond

Life can be very difficult
sometimes we feel abandoned
how can God let bad things
happen to us
or those we love?

Most of us have many
questions for God
many starting with "why?"

Be at peace my brothers and sisters
ask always, "What can I learn here?"
seek to grow
move always forward
to the Light

trusting God's love
even when we don't
understand

Gift of Scent

Incense, perfume
sweet fragrance of flowers
puppies, babies
fresh mountain air
today I am grateful
for the scent of bread baking
and all the wonderful smells
that delight us each day

S avoring smells of Grandma's cooking
C andles of beeswax cheerfully burning
E njoying the fragrance of a pine forest
N ew baby's sweet smell
T ime stands still in a fragrance of love

People

P eople
E ach is unique to be honored
O nly fools expect perfection
P lease and thank-you work magic
L ove even the people you don't like
E veryone deserves respect

Magic Carpet

Carpet on the floor
I wonder if it's magic
Let's go for a ride

How Long Does It Take?

How long does it take
to be kind
to care
give a smile
to listen
without judgement
or a need to give advice?

You can make a difference
in someone's life today
give the gift of love
compassion
acknowledgment
show, if only for a moment
that your soul
recognizes their soul
as one of God's creations
filled with the Light
of His love

Not You, Not Me

Look in your mirror
and see me
for it is not you
rather me you see
and if you are really blessed
you will see neither
you or me
only We

How We "Should" Feel

Do not tell anyone
how they should
or should not feel
for our feelings
are uniquely our own.

Sometimes we just
need time and compassion
to experience
how we feel
with no need to justify
it to ourselves or others

I'm Afraid

Sometimes I'm afraid
I know you think that's not true

Look behind my mask

Exactly Who You Are

Young, witty, intense
open, humble, willing to be
exactly who you are
opening your heart
letting it shine
God's love for all
Beyond the end of time

New Commitments

Grasses tipped in frost
winter's drawing near
sleigh bells sound an extra ring
lighted candles give a special glow

A special time of year
to reflect, then prepare
for new commitments
rejoicing in those fulfilled
asking for strength and grace
to keep the ones made now.

Surrender to God's will
love all our Creator
as made

Too hard, you say
yet living a life
outside of the grace of God
is even more difficult

Lay down your burdens
at the feel of the Lord
God is love—pure love

There is none besides Him.

Unchanging Truth

Real wisdom
lasts through the ages
while knowledge changes
over time

Godly wisdom is truth
that does not change
unlike earthly knowledge
with its fallible, mercurial
ideas, wisdom received
through God's grace
is truth through the ages

The core truth
by which
I live is
God is Love
He wants us to love
as He does

Live by this truth
always acting from
a position of love
and watch your life
unfold in marvelous ways
for great is the glory
of our Lord.

No Hate

It is hard to live with hate
it's sly energy begins to cling
to all it touches, until soon
it seeps inside all it surrounds

Yet there is a Force
that disperses the Darkness
it is the Light of Love

I will keep my focus
on my Lord
and learn to love
to spread His Light
wherever I am
across all eternity

Chocolate Kisses

Chocolate kisses, please
combine two favorite things
Sweet love at its best

A Haven

Butterfly cocoon
Bear snug in his snug winter den
All need a time out

Halo of Gold

Golden halo hair
Peaches and crème complexion
Angel with dimples

Her ebony skin
Carries herself like a queen
All heads turn for her

Great beauty's a gift
Only if it starts inside
Let your soul shine through

Forever Free

Many kinds of prisons
Yet we can always be free
Souls are untethered

God's Mercy

Like spring rains that
water the land
my tears flow
from my disobedience
dark clouds cover my soul
I weep, I weep
Afraid to call His name

Yet God is merciful
He calls gently to me
knowing my heart
is repentant
that I have turned
from my wicked ways

Come, my child
be in my Light
walk in love
for I am your God
throughout all time

Head Noise

Who are you who fills my head
with grumbling complaints
harsh judgment of others
daily dark chatter that
hides the Light?

Be gone, sly one who
seeks my soul for
I am a child of the Light

Though I may stumble
like a toddler learning to walk
the Lord, my God
is ever near
to offer a helping hand

Great is the grace of our Creator.

Creator of All

Bottomless sea, sky without end
the Creator of All
is pure love without borders
we cannot perceive of His majesty

Let me be a simple child
how can one study
what cannot be understood
books filled with stories
I cannot comprehend

Do not give me rules
to follow for I follow only
the Divine voice within
the Light of my soul

Drop of Water

Drop of water
change to snow, ice, steam
rain, river, sea
yet remains a drop of water
miracles surround those
willing to see

God Is

God is
even when you say
He does not exist.
Are you afraid
to believe?

God is
with or without us
for who are we
to think He is not
just because we say so!

Preparing for War

Preparing for war
that kills the young men
of the world
wiping out generations
using resources for
the needs of life and land

War—the true definition
of insanity

Point of View

What if the words
used to describe others
always describes you?
Would you change
your point of view?

Just As It Is

Can I accept life
just as it is
to see its cycles
of ups and downs?

How bright is

my candle within?
Can I sing a morning song
give salutations to the morning sun
dance with the fairies
on full moon nights
find peace within
during stormy times?

Yes, with your love
which strengthens me
I can do all
that I am called to do
wrapped in serenity
knowing your love
is with me
beyond the end of time

Holy Moments

It is a holy moment
a halt in time when
everything turns into
what it is meant to be

When one's faith is
so strong that all
we normally can't see
is revealed to us

I want these holy moments
enduring faith
that allows God's presence

in all things to shine forth

Leave the Rest to God

Do not try to bend
the world to what
you think it should be

Do only as much
as you can do and
accept that's all
you can do
leave the rest to God.

Time of Before

Do not cling
to the time of before
let it go
as one would empty
soggy coffee grounds

Start fresh each morning
letting your cup of joy
overflow, fresh brewed
laughter spilling from
your lips without
even a reason why

Each moment is new

and so is all in it
even that which was old
renews itself in a world
that never stops changing

Dragonfly Ride

I lie upon the meadow bloom
with daisies in my hair
yonder go the cattle
tip-toeing in a row
above me butterflies
flit here and there

A blue-tipped dragonfly
hovers offering me a ride
I quickly hop inside
off we dart across the field
my eyes see through his
I feel the breeze of his wings
how lovely to be free

It has been many years
since those days of
summer fantasy
when I was a child
living in my world
filled with love
and serenity

Magic and Dreams

A life built on
magic and dreams
white lies and fantasy
I slip between the layers
dimensions of reality
know all is real
and nothing is, too

An old woman's body
sits in my chair
I left her long ago
silence now holds me
in its hand
as I ride
a star of winter snow

I laugh with glee
as they try to drag me back
to an unkind world
they call reality

Leave me be
I like it here
in my world of
serenity

Living My Life Again

Like a favorite book re-read
I'm living my life again

correcting the errors
I'm a little wiser now
visiting each place
to see what I failed to see

I erase harsh words
thoughtless deeds
put love where there
once was hate

I visit the life
again and again
changing
all I did wrong
and the hurt
that was done to me

At last I finished
rebuilt my life
into a perfect reality
where streets are gold
angels sing
in perfect harmony

My Job, My Work

Nine to five
I do my job
five days a week
year after year
but, oh the joy
I do my work

that feeds my soul
in the other time

How fortunate is he
whose job is his work
how free he must be
maybe I'll get it right
one day and this will be
be the same for me

The Gypsy Girl

Tambourines ring
with the bells on her ankles
her rainbow skirt swirls
as she dances around the fire
they clap to the beat of her song

The gypsy girl
with flowing hair
tells my fortune
under the harvest moon

I laugh with delight
as she guesses my dreams
assuring me all will go well
in my make-believe world
where dreams come true
if promised by a gypsy girl

Green

Green
green peace
I dive into the forest of green
smell the wet woods
damp from summer rain
leaves bursting with green
the floresta is alive
wraps me in her arms
holds me to her bosom
allowing me to fill
with the serenity
of abundant life and love.

Don't Say "I Love You"

I no longer say
I love you
tarnished, overused
words of liars who
manipulate, devour

Love was never meant
to be captured in words
how useless are words
to express the Divine

Now I will be love
become so filled with
the Holy Light
that all I do, touch

becomes sacred
for immersed in love
one unites completely
with our Creator
making words unnecessary
useless, absurd

I am love
that's all I need
to be

Free Will?

Free will
great illusion
does God have a plan
do I willing follow His guidance
I'm trading free will
for serenity
eternity

No See, No Hear

I no longer see
with my eyes
for I've learned
to see with my heart

I do not hear the
chatter of the world

for I am listening
to the Divine Voice within

The move I lose
the more I gain
for God gives me
gifts more precious
when I am
will to receive

Wolf in Disguise

Is this a good person
or a wolf in disguise?
I have been fooled
sometimes because
I wanted what
the sly one offered

Now I listen to
the prickle of my skin
the uneasiness I feel
the voice that whispers
BEWARE

Dear Lord, please help
me discern when
evil comes to capture me
protect me by teaching me
to listen to that sense
that danger is near

Tormentor or Teacher?

> I am the pain
> is a wave not
> part of the sea?
>
> Is pain my tormentor
> or teacher?
> I must decide
> from moment to moment.

More Than Empty Words

> Forgiveness is more
> than empty words
> it must include action
> a cleansing of your heart
> sincere desire for the person
> to have a good life
> indeed, all the good
> you wish for your life.

www.ingramcontent.com/pod-product-compliance
Lightning Source LLC
Chambersburg PA
CBHW022110040426
42450CB00006B/648